# ECHOES FROM THE HIGH PEAKS

## Adventures of Adirondack Youth

Written and Illustrated
by
Victor Lamoy

North Country Books, Inc.
Utica, New York

# ECHOES FROM THE HIGH PEAKS

ISBN 0-925168-52-1

Cover photo courtesy of John Winkler,
author of *A Bushwacker's View of the Adirondacks*,
and soon-to-be-published, *A Cherished Wilderness*.

**Library of Congress Cataloging-in-Publication Data**

Lamoy, Victor, 1919-
    Echoes from the high peaks / by Victor Lamoy.
        p.    cm.
    ISBN 0-925168-52-1 (alk. paper)
    1. Lamoy, Victor, 1919-   —Childhood and youth.
2. Adirondack Mountain Region (N.Y.)—Biography.
3. Country life—New York (State)—Adirondack Mountains
Region. I Title. II. Title: Bygone adventures of Adirondack youth
CT275L2577.A3    1996
974.7'504'902—dc20
[B]                                              96-16795
                                                    CIP

North Country Books, Inc.
311 Turner Street
Utica, New York 13501

*To my father, Clayton Lamoy, Sr.
and to my brother, Clayton, Jr.,
who were my two best friends,
this book is humbly dedicated.*

# Foreword

After this lapse of years, I cannot claim that my memory of all the events and mode of life mentioned here are exact in detail. But the passages in this book, descriptive of times, places and persons involved, are as accurately described as memory permits.

The fundamental intention of this narrative is to depict the posture of youth during stressful times, living adventurously, while maintaining parental respect and concern for nature's wonders.

If you close your eyes to think of the past, just imagine the back of the eyelids to be a motion picture screen, displaying memories of precious and adventurous episodes in life, brought forth as a treasure known to you, and you alone. These are your jewels.

# Chapter 1

The water is lightly lapping at the back of my boots as I cast my wet flies down and across the gently flowing current of the renowned East AuSable. This celebrated trout stream pauses now and then in its northward journey to receive generous reinforcement from creeks along its banks. It is now five times its original width as it leaves the AuSable Lakes, and merrily joins the equally famous West AuSable, continuing on to fulfill the needs of its host, Lake Champlain.

Fishing with artificial flies, has for many years, been my favorite summer pastime, although, at times I revert to live bait when conditions dictate. I make up my own streamer and bucktail flies, which imitate minnows, and leave the more sophisticated imitations to the experts.

This seemingly endless tranquility remains though the fall, when an array of colorful hues is reluctantly deposited by the deciduous growth along the AuSable's banks. As winter quiets the murmur of the stream with its frigid influence, all is serene under the blanket of snow.

Then spring arrives, and with it, rising waters from the melting snow and ice. The water becomes a liberated catalyst in the impending havoc caused by the breakup of the icy mantle that has imprisoned it. Its innate characteristics have succumbed to the pressure of the crystalline flows crowding and bumping their way downstream. They show no mercy in their relentless nudging of defiant structures and in the probing of their glacial lumps over the banks, inundating yards and buildings with destructive indifference. Then, as its inordinate whim has been satisfied, the water recedes, exposing its moraine-like deposits.

Now, as the complacent stream surrounds me, it again murmurs pleasantly, as if expressing remorse for the seasonal flair of its boisterous behavior. A kingfisher sails overhead, uttering its piercing cry, while it seeks out a small trout or minnow, and I continue my fly casting, slowly moving downstream.

This now peaceful guise congers up thoughts of an earlier time when, in this same spot, native trout were abundant, and with their insatiable appetites provided sumptuous rewards to both novice and professional anglers.

While in this pensive mood, I gazed longingly across the stream at a hilly, brush-strewn pasture and envisioned the spectral appearance of a whitetail doe and twin fawns frolicking about, heedless of my presence.

This was the time of my adventurous youth. In this reflective state of mind, I find it appropriate to reveal the events of my young life, with its unique qualities and exciting escapades.

# Chapter 2

Growing up in the Adirondack Mountains of New York was an adventure in itself, especially during that provocative, yet quiescent period of the 1930's.

During the pre-depression era, my family operated a tourist home and restaurant which flourished during late spring, summer, and early fall. The business was begun when a new church was built and the old one, next door, was sold to the highest bidder—my dad.

After several months of tedious work, with the assistance of carpenters, plumbers and electricians, the structure was converted to its new image, "Clayton's Restaurant & Tourist Home." The new building was replete with eight bedrooms, two bathrooms, kitchen, dining space for more than sixty patrons and an eight-foot-wide porch across the front, facing both the street and river. From the comfortable chairs, one could relax while watching the AuSable swishing by, or just sit and inhale the invigorating mountain air. There was a gasoline pump in the rear for the guests' convenience, at nineteen cents a gallon.

We moved in in the spring, leaving the home where my younger brother, Clayton Jr. (we all called him Junior), and I were born just a very few years before. Our paternal grandmother volunteered for kitchen duty, with no objections from us! Mother and Dad ran the business which thrived from the beginning and soon required hired help. There were times when people streamed in and out all evening, so a makeshift cot was improvised under a kitchen cabinet where Junior and I would sleep for two or three hours until someone was free to put us to bed.

It was in the spring of my first year in school when the wonderful young mother we had hardly known became seriously ill with a rare strain of influenza. In those days, evaluating a medical situation was left in the hands of the family physician, and seldom was a patient admitted to a distant hospital unless an operation was mandatory, or a person was seriously injured. Our doctor ascertained that it was more favorable to keep Mother at home, where he could visit frequently, and she could have the family's attention.

3

It appeared evident that there was little or no improvement when the doctor's visits occurred more often, and my brother and I were only allowed to see Mother from her bedroom door.

Then that fateful day came when our loving mother was taken from us. I will never forget that sorrowful time when Grandmother took Junior and me into Mother's room, where she was temporarily propped up in bed with a glass tube protruding from lips that tried to smile as she caressed our outstretched hands. At that moment, in our young hearts and minds, we somehow know that she was saying goodbye.

In retrospect, I feel that, had there been antibiotics of some nature available then, she could have been a prudent influence in our lives in the years ahead.

Our dad was strong-willed, sagacious and understanding during this stressful time. His relations with us were reflective of our paternal grandmother, who provided the affection and guidance that was interrupted so abruptly and in such a woeful manner. Paternal grandfather died before Dad and Mother were married, and the maternal one while we were very young. Those of us left became a closely knit foursome, interdependent on each other.

# Chapter 3

Early in our lives, Junior and I became delightfully excited when Dad began taking us hunting and fishing. We were soon able to go fishing by ourselves, but serious hunting was more surrealistic, since being a season hunter was to be nurtured for several years. We were to learn about firearms safety, practical experience in wildlife activity, and the adherence to regulations concerning the environment.

As a precursor to our introduction to the magnificent forest, Dad would occasionally take us along on a stalking deer hunt. We three, with our warm and colorful attire, seemed to melt into the pristine fall environment. My brother and I felt so inviolable, yet submissive to the overpowering influence of nature—we two, with our Daisy air-rifles, following our magnanimous leader. I envisioned a time in the near future when we would proudly display our hunting licenses and traipse off into the wilderness with great enthusiasm. We would not forget to utilize the skills taught us by our diligent and patient parent.

One of our excursions that began auspiciously, but proved to be an integral part of our wildlife education, shall forever be instilled in my memory.

We were walking single file as usual, watching, waiting, and then pressing on alternately, as silently as possible, when Dad came to a halt and raised his hand to signal caution as he had done many times before. In a flash, a large whitetail doe and her two half-grown fawns bounded up the steep mountainside through the open timber, their white flags jauntily bidding farewell as they passed. Their exit seemed more pretentious than fearful, as if they were aware that we would not harm them. It was a buck that Dad was after and immediately surmised that one could very well be in the area.

After a short pause to allow the deer to quiet down, we proceeded painstakingly in the direction the three had taken toward the summit until we found signs that  they had altered their course. They were bearing off to one side, so that the prevailing breeze would be in their favor. With the realization that it would prove useless to continue the pursuit, we headed up to the crown of the predominantly oak-timbered ridge, which showed conspicuous signs of deer activity.

We slunk unobtrusively across the ridge to a rocky ledge that dropped off into a valley of small trees and brush, before continuing up through the full-grown timber of the mountainside. The mountain, named Saddleback due to its shape, was the victim of a bad fire several years before, but had bounced back with lush new greenery.

As we studied the rough, rocky side of the admirable mount, there came a veritable explosion below us as a magnificently antlered patriarch of the forest leaped from his hiding place and bounded through the dense evergreens and underbrush. Dad got off two shots with his .32 caliber semi-automatic, but knew that they were ineffective. The buck had his avenue of escape pre-planned, and used it to his advantage.

As the excitement waned and we were about to investigate the disappearance of that beautiful animal, I took a final exasperated glance at old Saddleback. There, behind a large rotten log, about half-way of the rugged mountainside, stood a giant black bear, with one paw clinging to a small birch tree. I pointed and stammered, "Dad, look!" He remarked that his shots at the buck must have roused the bear. It seemed to be about 300 yards away, quite a long range for the .32, Dad judged, as he took aim and fired. The bear was clearly hit as he shook that little birch violently before falling, at which time he tore the rotten log apart, kicking it down the mountainside. Dad gave the animal another round that sent him lurching into the brushy growth toward a notch at the end of the mountain. Dad reloaded his rifle and we proceeded to where he had last seen the bear. "Keep your eyes peeled," Dad warned. "He may not have gone far."

The rough terrain made progress haltingly slow. There were old, rotted remnants of a sluiceway used many years before to float pulpwood, cut from the mountain's virgin timber, to the river miles below. The sluice water was abundantly supplied by mountainside springs and brooks. There were jagged rocks with out-croppings of juniper, young spruce, balsam, and hemlock. The forest fire that devastated hundreds of acres of native growth had left scars of black stumps and tree stubs, now partially hidden by small evergreens and wild ferns.

It was into this mass of unfamiliar and impregnable hodgepodge that the bear escaped. Each time we noticed a black stump partly obscured by evergreens, our hearts were in our

6

mouths. Dad was continually on the alert, and Junior and I were beginning to suggest what we would do should the wounded bear, in a final act of malice, decide to claw us to shreds. That's when Dad decided that one rifle-toting adult, two kids with B-B guns, and a wounded bear added up to less than a fortuitous situation! His solution to the dilemma was "Let's get the h- - - out of here!"

The following day Dad, with a couple of other seasoned hunters, picked up from where we had so willingly departed. They found where the bear had wandered into a mud wallow, and as often happens we learned, sealed its wounds by rolling in the healing balm of Mother Earth.

There's no substitute for experience, we are told, so I would assume that Junior and I consumed a whole volume in our young lives, in just one day! But little did we realize then, what was in store for us in the future!

# Chapter 4

Fishing is one of the most popular outdoor sports for people of all ages, but unfortunately for many, active participation is limited. It was a major source of pleasure in our youth, the AuSable River being a stone's throw away. This celebrated trout stream that gurgled assiduously through our little hamlet provided an abundance of brown, rainbow, and brook trout to those with patience and a little determination. Proficiency abounded among those professional anglers who sported the sophisticated equipment and lures. Often, they were representatives of tackle companies engaged in testing their products. Our tourist home provided the lodging.

Of course, Junior and I both admired and envied them, but to placate our avid desire to possess even a minute part of their skills, we accepted the fact that, for the present, it was out of our league. For now, it would be in our dream world.

When spring came with its liberation of the stark, dormant northern environment, my brother and I began anticipating the long-awaited opening of fishing season—May 1st. The days dragged on until, finally, the unpredictably stubborn ice succumbed to the enlivening rays of the sun and reluctantly broke apart, uncompromising in its turbulent journey. This was the high point of our hopes for an early spring.

"Worms! Worms!" Junior would frantically exclaim. "We gotta have worms!" With the evocative air of urgency dominating the verbal onslaught, it was evident that a search for unfrozen earth was forthcoming. Grandmother believed it too early to spade up the vegetable garden plot, but didn't object, primarily because she knew very well this unctuous behavior would not to be so eagerly displayed come planting time!

We dug up an area in one corner of the garden, and found a sufficient number of fat earthworms for the time being, storing them in a container of soil and covering with a perforated metal lid.

Night-crawlers are best spotted late at night, on closely-mown lawns and golf courses. We found a few large night-crawlers under some moist leaves shed by a nearby maple last fall. Those giant worms made enticing lures for large brown trout, rainbows, or lake trout, when hooked behind a spinner or string of spoons. Big bait, big fish, we thought!

Though my brother and I had an annual penchant for the first day of fishing season to fall on a weekend, it seldom obliged. We always had our fishing rods assembled the night before, snelled hooks and sinkers attached, and our bait resting comfortably behind the kitchen stove.

A restless night, disturbed by visions of monster trout, would abruptly end when Grandmother shook us into consciousness, making a somewhat harsh remark, "C'mon, foolhardy kids. Imagine getting up this early just to go fishin'!"

Regardless of Grandmother's seeming displeasure, there was hot oatmeal and golden brown toast waiting, which was eagerly washed down with hot Ovaltine. We then donned warm clothes and boots, and headed for the river. Grandmother reminded us that she would get us in one hour to get spruced up for school, which fortunately was close by. What a disgusting thought, we concurred, but perhaps the hour could be stretched a little bit!

Our customary location on the river bank, just below the mouth of a large brook and a few yards upstream from an iron bridge spanning the river, was partially inundated by the high, roiled water. Fragments of ice floes that defiantly resisted the sun's influence made cumbersome obstacles to climb or slide over. Undeterred by the adverse conditions, our lines were quickly in the spirited stream and our expectations high.

Periodically we checked our baited hooks, changed positions on the river bank, and set our rods down while we warmed our cold, wet hands in our jacket pockets. After a time it became evident that the icy water had not only discouraged the trout from biting, but was causing quite a bit of distress on our part. It just wasn't our day! Perhaps some other time, when it's warmer, the trout would be biting.

We didn't protest when Dad appeared by the railing on the bridge and beckoned us. Just as we were leaving, Junior pointed out a first robin in the large elm tree over our heads. I looked up, too late to see a white blob coming down. Thank goodness, I didn't have my mouth open, for it landed on my chin! Both Dad and Junior had a roaring good laugh over that, but I warned my brother to keep his yap shut about it in school, if he cared to avoid becoming fish bait! Grandmother thought it was funny too!

This early spring ritual lasted for several years, and became a lasting memory from our young lives. We eventually evolved into seasoned anglers, with thanks to our dad, who took us to distant streams, lakes and ponds, where we often camped out overnight. Having Dad as our mentor, we learned the importance of using our inherent qualities, and the need to respect human values and nature's distinctive traits.

# Chapter 5

It was a year or more after the disastrous stock market debacle of 1929, that the tourist business began to reveal itself in an uncompromising way. It trickled down to an occasional visitor, the income from which would hardly pay the electric bill! It seemed strange to us kids that things couldn't go on as before, but we sensed that something was afoot. There was no relief provided, as is predominate today; you had to make it on your own, one way or another, or sink into complete poverty.

Stocking the kitchen with food for guests was not feasible, when the guests were few and far between. Occasionally a restaurant patron would place an order for soup and a sandwich, or something simple, which we generally could provide. But, if an order came for steak, ground beef, pork chops or something of that nature, one of us scurried to the grocery next door with a note from Grandmother. After the customer had paid the bill and left, someone retraced the steps to the store and paid the bill there. The net profit? Maybe thirty cents! But that would buy three large loaves of bread or a pound of the best ground beef.

It became evident that living conditions were not going to improve in the near future, and that it would be necessary to find a means of becoming more self-sufficient. We had a half-acre lot behind the place, so why not be practical and farm it?

The thought of having animals around was exciting for us. This enthusiastic vein would soon disappear when we became aware of certain aspects of farming.

Grandmother had always nurtured a vegetable garden and was proficient in utilizing the space to the fullest. Other than cooking, baking and our welfare, her horticultural activities prevailed. In addition to the usual produce from her organic kingdom, we picked wild berries of all species, which were canned along with other preserves. Some items were either pickled or salted to keep from spoiling. Frozen food was not popular, except in late fall when beef, pork, and venison were kept outdoors in their natural state until consumed piecemeal by spring. Dad never failed to keep a good supply of venison on hand.

11

In early spring, Dad somehow obtained a guernsey cow that was just about ready to calve. He hastily constructed a stall for it in the partitioned garage. As soon as the cow had her calf, she produced lots of milk. When the little one learned to drink from a pail, it was given to the farmer who supplied the cow—and everyone was happy. That is, except the "you-know-whos" that cleaned up behind!

Then came a half-dozen chickens to feed and eggs to gather, most times under protest from the chickens. Somehow a pig that had no premonition of its future, appeared in a pen adjacent to the garden. It squealed incessantly until one of us scratched its back. Dad and Grandmother frowned on us making a pet of it, and some of their remarks made us a bit suspicious of its future, something about "the little porker becoming ham and chops." Junior and I just couldn't visualize such a dastardly act!

One thing that made this little pig unique was its tail. It wasn't curly as it should have been, but perfectly straight, and wagging like a dog's! Nobody in the area had ever heard of such a quality. Being adventurous, I sent a vivid description of the animal to "Ripley's Believe-It-Or-Not."

I had completely erased the item from my memory until the next spring, when I began receiving post cards from persons in different parts of the country, asking for pictures of the "pig with the straight tail." I couldn't very well reply when, not prescient of the article's reception, the adult hog had been butchered and devoured before the item was published!

While on the subject of swine, I feel it appropriate to reveal an incident which indirectly involved pigs and a man named Andy, who did a major share of the butchering in the area.

The old gent was an ominous appearing character, which appropriately fit his seasonal occupation. He was a mild-mannered, well-liked individual and would never harm anyone. He did, however, enjoy scaring kids with his butcher knife, and/or bloody hands after one of his jobs.

Early one fall evening I was delivering a neighbor's newspaper a short distance up a side street, when, at the corner of the main street, I met Andy. It was apparent that he had just finished one of his jobs. He laughed in a raucous tone as he extended his bloodied hands toward me. I immediately lost all sense of being, took an exit into the street and into the front fender of a Ford sedan!

I have no idea how much damage the car sustained, as I

only became conscious some time later; the family and our doctor hovering over me. Other than a few stitches here and there, a lump on the head and a sore collarbone, I was in pretty good shape. The doctor, who was a dedicated General Motors customer, remarked that had it been any car but a Ford that hit me, I would have been dead!

The owner of the Ford was a bobsled driver from Lake Placid, who kept in touch for months after the accident. Later, in the winter, he gave me a thrilling ride down the future Olympic Bobsled Run at Mt. Hovenberg.

I felt sorry for old Andy. He never seemed to fully get over the experience, but he gave up scaring kids and washed his hands before he took to the street.

Getting back to our "little farm," Pansy, our guernsey cow, was producing a pail of milk twice a day. From the cream, Grandmother made butter and cottage cheese. The by-product of churning, buttermilk, was eagerly consumed by the older folks, but there was no craving for it on my part!

During the summer, Pansy spent her days lazily enjoying a lush green pasture. A few hundred yards across a highway, a brook and then through a gate, took her to her Utopia. In late afternoon she would be patiently waiting for the return trip, with the characteristic lowing that greeted our arrival. Junior was a bit lighter than me, and was allowed to ride the bovine back and forth, to and from the barn, while I led her by a rope tied to her halter. She never objected to the clinging rider.

During the winter, Pansy stayed in the barn and caused more work feeding, watering and cleaning up behind. The latter is where the lack of enthusiasm mentioned before became obvious, but we intended to do our part, despite the offensive nature of the task.

# Chapter 6

When I was ten years old and Junior a little over eight, we noticed that Dad was spending more time away from home than before. The main reason, we ascertained, was that he was being detained by his Watkins Products customers. Then a rather unexpected relationship appeared with a comely lass, who later became our stepmother.

Hazel and Grandmother were compatible in most respects, and though Hazel never interfered with the customary procedures set down previously, she was always eager to offer suggestions. Her relationship with we two was as genial as could be expected at first, but in time she became very dear to us.

The business was beginning to improve to the extent that, with the meager income from the product sales, along with a mail run from our town to AuSable Forks, we were able to dispense with the farm animals. During Dad's Saturday afternoon mail run, my brother and I would often attend a matinee at the Bridge Theater. For ten cents, we could watch western movies with Tom Mix, or Tarzan of the Apes, Charlie Chan and others of that nature. Dad would usually come into the theater and sit out the finish.

Uncle Leslie, Dad's brother, came to live with us for awhile about this time, and agreed to share expenses. It seems that he had lost his job with a painting contractor, as well as having been ejected by his wife. It was just a slight misunderstanding, he explained, and the contentious provocation would soon blow over. When after several months there was no sign of reparation, it was obvious that he didn't intend to alter the situation. While "boarding" with us, he worked at house painting at irregular times and in various locations. It was eventually discovered that some of his earnings were converted to a liquid form at a friend's illegal home brewery, his manner of walking and talking congruent with his condition.

In spite of Uncle Leslie's unsteady, tipsy behavior after the paint and brushes were retired for the day, his work was beyond reproach. He was often sought out by patrons who were familiar with his ability and artistic traits. Uncle Les could mix and match colors compatible with just about any given situation, using his sixth-sense knack of perception. He once painted a sign for a meat market, which also portrayed some choice items. I heard later from one who had admired the art work, that the ham appeared authentic enough to cut off a slice!

One time my uncle mentioned that he believed me to be somewhat artistically inclined, but I shrugged it off as an excuse to inveigle me into helping him with his work. His persistent, yet suave manner finally won me over, but I just couldn't perceive what connection clapboards had to do with art! At least it was valuable experience, and he handed me a couple of bucks now and then, which was a fortune for an eleven-year-old kid!

His faith in me was, most likely, responsible for my interest in art later in life, when I studied illustrating and cartooning. Had I depended solely on that as my life's work, however, I'm sure that I would have starved.

Other than the painting, the summer work for us kids was usually mowing lawns with the old reel-type push mowers, weeding Grandmother's backyard produce development and doing simple chores around the house. I mowed lawns once a week for two brothers, Frank and Charlie. Frank had a large estate that matched his wallet, while Charlie had a much smaller piece of greenery and had to depend upon a less fulfilling life style. When Frank's job was finished, he graciously handed me fifty cents, while Charlie gave me a dollar, along with a compliment. It wasn't difficult to understand how Frank gained his opulence!

Maintaining good relations with our benefactors made our existence tolerable and gave Junior and I a certain amount of flexibility in coming and going, up to a point. In summer we played baseball, went fishing, swimming and hiking with the kids in our age group.

We were not alone in the need for a more prolific life-style. Need was widespread through our region, and many families were in much worse condition than we. At least we still had our home, although it took practically all of our skimpy income to keep it operating.

Though young and irresponsible, my brother and I were constantly aware how difficult life can become. We didn't ask for things we knew were out of reach when we could perceive the pain in the eyes of those who couldn't bestow them upon us. We were assured of the importance our lives made in the destiny of a strong-willed family, and we felt admiration for the moral and steadfast qualities that would make our survival a positive reality. From this we learned the value of being loved and cared for, with the unselfish sacrifices of our capable benefactors.

Back in the early part of the summer, I had noticed that Hazel was beginning to gain weight around the waist. She didn't seem to be eating much, even when we were all just barely getting by on single helpings! We kids ate what was put before us, whether we liked it or not, because that's all we had and there was no wasted food. Whatever scraps were left went to our faithful dog, Sport, who would eat anything that was chewable, like an old football, shoe or piece of wood!

In early August came the answer to the mystery of Hazel's gaining weight. Although we had been a bit suspicious, after a short stay in the Neighborhood Clinic, Hazel brought us a baby brother named Robert. He appeared healthy in every way, but later on developed eczema, which for many months forced him to wear home-made cotton mittens to prevent digging at the itchy areas.

Now Junior and I, the learned ones, found in him an outlet for our superior knowledge. There would be many questions, but did we have all the answers? Only time would tell some years in the future.

During the fleeting summer, in addition to our boyhood activities, we had begun to notice certain individuals of the opposite sex in a different light. They just didn't seem to be as repulsive or baffling as before. After the school sessions got under way in early fall, it wasn't at all uncommon to be aware of a certain amount of suppressed emotion toward each other.

An attractive ten-year-old lass, whom I will call Marie, had been occupying my thoughts since mid-summer when we met at a church picnic. On the pretext of one thing or another, we were able to maintain a compatible relationship, which endured the derisive comments of indignant youngsters for quite some time. A few adolescents were accusing us of imaginary proclivity, when there was not a snippet of logic in their basis of opinion. We liked each other's company and were good friends, but in later years varied life-styles caused us to drift apart. It was a pleasant and rewarding experience that prepared me for the future.

# Chapter 7

Toward the end of October, Dad was invited to spend a weekend at a hunting camp with a cousin, Jim Maynard. It was located on state land near a large private park. I guess Dad must have mentioned that he was considering taking Junior and I for an outing because Jim countered with, "Bring them along, they'll enjoy it!"

To us, this was not unlike the excitement we experienced before the first day of fishing season. Though the fifty-mile trip was not to materialize for a few days yet, we were beside ourselves with anticipation, and a medley of preparations fit for an African safari was beginning to take form. We couldn't grasp the placid, unruffled attitude of our father when there was so much at stake in this venture!

We had participated in a significant number of hunting trips with Dad previously, but we were never as excited as with this prospect of spending a couple of days and nights at camp.

Sleeping bags were not a part of our meager inventory, but extra blankets, pillows and plenty of warm clothing were packed and ready to go after school on Friday. Grandmother had prepared some extra provisions for the camp larder, which would be a token of our appreciation for the invitation. Hazel was asked to go along, but politely declined on the basis of Bobbie's disorder, and there was canning to finish.

It was nearly six in the evening when our car left the main highway and wound down a one-lane dirt road for over a mile. After crossing a plank bridge over a small brook, there was the camp nestled in the sanctuary of tall, majestic spruce trees. Even from outside, it appeared warm and snug. The outward appearance did not belie rustic charm of its interior.

This type of camp was built by permit from the State, on State land and to State specifications. It was designed as a temporary shelter, to be used at the permit-holder's discretion. A leveled wood platform with solid sidewalls four or five feet high supported the rafters, usually made up of poles or rough two-by-fours. These were fastened to the sidewalls and ridge pole.

The framework was then covered with chicken wire and that, in turn, provided a sag-proof surface to receive the waterproofed canvas roof. Many of these camps that were occupied from early spring to late fall, used an additional canvas tarp (tent fly) over the original to furnish added protection from the elements. A door with a glass insert was used at the front gable end, a small window at the rear.

At the end of the fall hunting season, the canvas and moveable objects were removed for the winter, leaving the framework as a lifeless monument to fond memories.

Jim's wife Mary met us at the door, explaining that Jim and a close friend, Earl, were probably on their way in from watching for deer at particular runways. By the time we unloaded our gear and arranged our equipment, Jim and Earl arrived. They had seen several deer, but none with antlers.

Mary had already prepared a large pot of venison stew, the alluring waft of which made one hungrier by the minute! It was soon placed before us and readily devoured, topped off by generous hunks of Grandmother's mouth-watering chocolate cake.

Junior and I helped Mary clean up while Dad, Jim and Earl were discussing methods of outwitting the wily bucks. From this, tales evolved of previous, more or less successful game hunts, including Dad's account of the hunt for a wounded bear, with two kids armed with air-rifles! My brother and I were proud to be a part of it, though scared out of our wits at the time.

During the conversation, a vehicle could be heard approaching from the direction of the main highway. As it pulled into the parking area in front, Jim glanced out the door glass and announced, "It's the game warden!" Then, in the next breath he whispered, "Somebody cover that pack-basket over there in the corner!"

I had noticed that a towel had been draped over the container, but had no idea as to its contents. Earl stepped over to it and sat on top, as Jim welcomed our visitor and invited him in. There were the usual introductions, and some conversation ensued as to the hunter's luck, the weather, the deer population—idle chatter. We noticed that Earl seemed to be quite uncomfortable and shifted his weight at short intervals, but couldn't understand his painful expression.

After the verbal exchange had died down, Mary offered the warden a piece of cake, which he eagerly devoured, wished us luck and left. As soon as his vehicle backed out and headed down the road, Earl, with an air of relief, bounced to his feet. There, protruding from the top of the pack-basket, was a deer's hoof that had been centered on his posterior! It was no wonder that he was distressed!

It was then explained that the hoof was part of the hind quarter of a small deer that someone shot by mistake and left in the woods. In not allowing the meat to be wasted, Jim brought part of the carcass into camp—hence the venison stew. We all agreed this was a situation that could not justifiably be explained to a game warden.

We turned in for the night some time after ten, to be rested for an early rise come morning. Junior and I had an upper bunk next to the slanted roof, while Dad occupied the lower. On the opposite side, Earl took the upper, over Jim and Mary's three-quarter bed below. The lamps were extinguished, everyone uttered "good night" and all was quiet except for the subdued crackle of the wood fire and the occasional hoot of an owl. The rustic "bathroom" was a cold journey by flashlight to the outside, several yards behind the camp.

It seemed only a short interval until the announcement of "It's daylight in the swamp" jolted us into consciousness. Five a.m. already? The wood fire was stoked up, while my brother and I fetched a couple of pails of water from the brook. We had warm water from the night before to wash up with, thank goodness, for that brook water was ice cold!

As always in camp, one's taste buds become excited just by the hint of food, and when the cooking begins, it's all out for whatever is on the menu. Could it be psychological? I doubt it!

As far as the hunting went, Junior and I were both too young to be very deeply involved, although the subject was one of our most important plans for the future. With the outings shared with Dad, we learned the basic do's and don'ts, and were preseasoned by the time we were allowed to carry rifles.

Now we could only be tag-alongs and enjoy the association with our elders, which delighted us immensely. That morning Junior was going out with Dad, and I with Jim; Earl was taking the north trail which led to the junction of an adjoining private park. After walking, sitting and watching for almost three hours, we headed back to camp for a midday rest. At that time of day the deer are inactive, but move around later to feed.

During the midday lull, Junior and I were appointed to use

our excess energy to convert some existing logs into firewood. Using a sawbuck and crosscut saw, we used the you-pull, I-pull method on the hard and soft wood logs. We had a several day's supply before lunch, then rested up awhile to prepare for our afternoon tag-along.

While participating in this outing with the "pros" and their stalking activities, my thoughts were idly filled with wonder and awe. How many other kids our age could be as fortunate as we? Being able to immerse one's thoughts and actions into this marvelous fulfillment of a dream involving life and nature was a rarity indeed!

It was getting toward dusk when we started back to camp. There had been others hunting in the outlying areas, which explained the earlier sound of distant rifle shots, some perhaps successful, more that were not. One of the earlier reports which sounded relatively close, turned out to be about Dad, who downed a wandering spike-horn buck. He and Junior got it gutted out and dragged into camp before we arrived. Mary used her deer tag to make it legal, as she didn't intend to hunt anyway. It also provided an excuse for having venison in camp, which was a relief to Earl.

We enjoyed another deliciously filling meal, relaxation and hunting stories, then a restful night. Sunday morning was wet and cold, making it undesirable to get out, so we slept a little later, then packed for home.

It had been another delightful and educational experience— one that we hoped would come again at that comfortable shelter, and with those wonderful people.

# Chapter 8

With winter approaching our mountainous habitat, we could rely on the climate's cold northwest winds, snow and ice. With the economy at an all-time low, the older generation, through years of experience, prepared their families many months in advance. There was a stocking-up program with homegrown, canned and preserved food, as well as new, warm clothing ordered from Sears Roebuck, in whatever categories fit the meager budget.

There had been a significant amount of knitting accomplished in the preceding months which produced wool socks, mittens, scarves, and toques. By November, we had replaced our undershorts with fleece-lined one-piece underwear, having the indispensable, and crucial, flap in the back. The garment also served as a sleeping and lounging suit, being changed twice a week, after the semi-weekly bath.

As we progressed in age and self-proclaimed perfection to a level above, we began to detest the use of that unfashionable underwear unless we were involved in outdoor sports or other activities. Although we bitterly protested, it fell on deaf ears, until a later time when we were involved in school sports programs.

Outdoor sports were the envy of those not blessed with the frigid thermometer readings, deep snow and ice—always ice. Most of the local youngsters participated in some activity or sport. There was skating, skiing, bobsledding, ski jumping, tobogganing, ice hockey and variations of each, plus some daring innovations that would turn parents into nervous wrecks! Those antics were not performed on purpose—they just came naturally.

When the river was snow-free, we took special delight in skating over surfaces where the water could be seen flowing an inch or two underneath. At those times when the ice was bare, we would skate up and down the river for a mile or more. Occasionally, a reckless one of us would come speeding back, coated with ice from head to toe, having broken through and gotten wet.

When snowfall covered the river ice, skating was limited to

small areas that could be cleared repeatedly by those who felt ambitious with snow shovels. Usually the wind would blow the snow right back!

To the rescue came "Uncle" Louie, who owned and operated an Italian restaurant of the east side of the river. With the help of his talented son and others who sympathized with our cause, he built a regulation hockey rink, complete with backboards, lighting and equipment, behind the establishment. He also converted an old shed into a warm shelter where we could don our skates and store extra clothing. This project was a benefit to him, when parents, spectators and members of other teams patronized his business.

Dad wasn't very happy about having his sons beaten up with hockey sticks, or maimed by a wayward puck, but gave in when I mentioned that I might otherwise go for football next fall. The goalie was the only one with protection, which consisted of a baseball catcher's vest and mask, shin guards and heavy leather gloves. The players wore sweatshirts and shorts, thigh-length part-wool stockings, and wool socks. Head protection amounted to one colorful wool knit toque. In retrospect, Dad's concern was not unfounded!

Two teams were organized, one being comprised of eleven to thirteen-year-olds, and the other fourteen through nineteen. The older team was named "The Tigers" and our junior team aptly called "The Cubs."

Other teams in the area were also fortunate in having interested sponsors, providing imposing competition. My position was at right wing, which I fulfilled faithfully and with a certain amount of enjoyment. As time passed, the games seemed to become more austere and the players imbued with malice, which made the fun fade—but that is hockey!

After having been battered senseless with a hockey stick, and then having stopped a ninety-mile-per-hour puck with my ankle, which laid me up for almost two weeks, I decided to try something less dangerous such as ski jumping or bobsledding, for my winter recreation. By the first of February, however, I was back on the ice.

As a follow-up to the Winter Olympic Games in Lake Placid, a Winter Pageant was planned for mid-February. Four of us twelve and thirteen-year-old skaters were selected to play a part, which entailed several evenings of practice at the Olympic Area.

We were to escort Sonja Henie, the Norwegian Olympic

Gold Medal Figure Skating Champion, to the center of the ice in a gold chariot (on runners), two of us on each side. Upon alighting from her conveyance, we four, dressed in white uniforms with green capes and carrying mock trumpets, would raise our instruments (a musician in the orchestra did the notes), then we would return to the entrance gate. It all worked out perfectly.

Upon finishing her program, we returned to the center of the arena, circling her with the chariot. I then assisted her into the royal conveyance and we returned to the gate. Then came the best part—that beautiful, smiling figure gave each of us an appreciative hug!

There was just one indication of a potential problem, that only I was aware of. Before I took to the ice on the trip out, I had loosened my skate laces to straighten the tongues, and had no time to tighten them. The cuffs of the white trousers covered the dangling strings that were so crucial in keeping the skates tight and ankles stiff. How I ever managed to keep from fouling up the performance, I'll never know! The one thing I was sure of, was that I had laced skates on the final trip!

The most popular sledding spot in our immediate area was none other than a paved street that rose more than thirty feet in elevation over a length of several hundred yards. The one critical problem here was dodging traffic. Sliding after dark was one solution, as the autos were less likely to be on the street, and those that were displayed headlights easily recognized from a safe distance away. Then there was the intersection with the main street, where I had the one-sided argument with the Ford sedan a couple of years previously. At that corner, the street continued over a bridge to the east side of the river.

This required a spotter—usually a parent, or responsible adult, to relay the all-clear to another person half-way up the hill. When the sleds came speeding down at more than 30 miles-per-hour, depending upon the base, they glided across the bridge and coasted to a stop several yards beyond, near Uncle Louie's. Some of the parents enjoyed this as much as the kids, for we could hear their happy shrieks as they sailed by us on the kid's Flexible Flyers.

The family that lived closest to us, with our backyards joining, included two boys, Don and Russ. Their father worked as a maintenance man at the famous Lake Placid Club, while their mother managed the village telephone office in their home. Don was two years ahead of me in school, was an "A" student with an inventive mind, and a proponent of some outlandish ideas. In one instance I remember the experiment of eating an apple while suspended upside down, hanging from a trapeze bar, to prove that it is possible to swallow uphill!

Recalling that I had ridden a bobsled down the Olympic bob run, and stating that sliding down the street hill was for amateurs, Don concluded that we should make a two-man bobsled. Using their woodshed for a workshop, we began to assemble odds and ends of old lumber, car parts and hardware, plus two old dilapidated Flexible Flyer sleds. After about three weeks of after-school and Saturdays (no one but farmers worked on Sundays), we had constructed a reasonable, small-scale replica of an Olympic bobsled.

It had an old auto steering wheel at the end of a piece of pipe, a rope pulley at the lower end, and was covered with a metal cowling. This mechanism moved the shortened front sled laterally to alter the direction of travel. The rear sled provided seating for two, the driver and the brakeman, whose job was to operate the two levers which, when pulled up and back, would dig in to slow or stop the sled.

After several fast runs down the street hill, with Don and I taking turns at driving, we began searching for a more gratifying run, where speeds would be more challenging for our "sophisticated" machine. Soon, we learned of a wooded mountain road that lumbermen were using as a means to transport logs down the steep incline. In looking it over, we discovered it to be a winding, but reasonably smooth path about six feet wide with icy patches at irregular intervals.

The following Saturday was a beautiful winter day, with the skidway free of loggers. This was the opportunity we had been waiting for.

With those who came to watch taking places along the trail, we pulled our sled up and up the slick incline to a pre-arranged starting point. We flipped a coin, with the result putting me in the driver's seat. I made it clearly understood that it was our maiden voyage down this untried course, and if I asked for brakes, I was to get brakes—immediately!

We pushed off, and after a couple hundred feet discovered that the run was rougher than imagined, and much faster! As we plummeted down the winding trail, the vibration was becoming more intense as the speed increased. The trees were a blur and it was imperative that I cut the turns shorter to allow a wider exit from them. We had several hundred feet of skid-way remaining to the flat below, when we hit a patch of ice on a long turn. I immediately realized that we were in trouble and yelled for the brakes! Don obeyed in seconds, but they didn't dig in evenly, making us careen off into the woods. Through flying snow we plowed, dodging trees and smashing brush, until abruptly halted by a large stump.

The steering mechanism was in pieces, my goggles were down around my neck, along with one of Don's legs, and his jacket was draped over his head. Although the sled was a complete mess, we were fortunate to have only a few bruises and scrapes, along with fractured egos and a few cheers from the spectators—cheers for still being alive!

Later, I asked Don if we should repair the sled and make some new adjustments to correct its faults, then try the run again. He looked at me with a puzzled expression and said, "Let's go skiing!"

Skiing was popular in those days, along with toboggan rides down open hills and sloped meadows. Lake Placid boasted having the fastest toboggan slide, which was built similar to a ski jump, with the exit in a trough that extended well out onto the ice of Mirror Lake.

Near home we had an area with a series of hills which became progressively smaller as one tobogganed down. The ride would take us over one hill, through the valley, up and down the next, and the next, to the flat below. We also skied diagonally from one hill to another.

The ski equipment used by my brother and me amounted to a pair of ash or hickory skis, and two bamboo ski poles each. There was no ski binding—only a rubber band cut from an old auto inner tube, stretched around the boot heel and under the front of the toe strap.

As far as we were concerned, they were masterful outfits that enabled us to succeed in performing some downhill exploits that are today described with glitzy phrases! Some of the other kids had more modern equipment, but we were not overly impressed by it. We all took tumbles—lots of tumbles, and in time experienced sprains and bruises, some of which made parents pray for the snow to disappear. The enjoyment was still there, nonetheless.

Ski jumping fascinated me to the point of addled admiration. There were others who had a fleeting interest in the sport, but nothing that would arouse anxiety. However, with a few skeptical volunteers and a long, steep hill, a ski jump was built about two-thirds of the way down the slope.

Using an existing large, flat rock as a departure point, we formed a chute with logs, old planks and packed snow. The point of lift-off was a little over three feet from the slope of the hill's lower incline but, depending upon the speed of descent and leg lift, we predicted a jump of fifteen or twenty feet should be possible.

I was unanimously selected for the trial run. I didn't intend to make a big thing of it by starting at the crest of the hill, therefore I came into the slope from the side, about half way up. I had discarded my makeshift ski harness and used only the toe straps for this perilous performance.

The lift-off was perfect, but then I wondered what I was supposed to do next! I leaned forward, and remained so, landing on my belly and chin, minus the skis that preceded me down the slope. I shuddered to think of the catastrophe had I come from the top of the hill! As a result, we all started low on the hill and gradually worked upward until, with spills galore, we mastered the jump with remarkable results for us kids!

# Chapter 9

Our parents' prayers had been answered! The snow was now rapidly disappearing, our daring feats subdued, and our elders' nerves more relaxed—for the time being.

Dad had been studying taxidermy with a Master Taxidermist, Frank Holt. Frank lived near a small village a few miles to the south. His excellence was the result of many years of tireless dedication to the art, but now he was ready to pass it on. He was thankful that Dad had shown such an interest in the work.

With Spring arriving, thoughts emerged of fishing and the need for a vehicle of some sort. But we were still too young to be burdened by all of those licenses that the state insisted on issuing and enforcing: hunting, fishing (if you were over 16), trapping and driving.

One warm day we removed some frozen snow and ice from a lump next to the back yard fence and, lo and behold, there appeared a Model T Ford engine! Now all we needed was a frame to mount it on, wheels with axles, a driveshaft, at least the front half of a car body, and an assortment of connections and do-dads!

With the help of our neighbors, Don and Russ, and a mechanically gifted friend named Albert, we began by getting the engine mounted on a pair of sawhorses, where it could be fitted with wiring, coil, a gas line, and other necessities.

It was still a couple of months before school would be out for the summer, making our search for suitable components restricted to our evenings, weekends, and when not otherwise involved in activities such as schoolwork and chores around the house.

Practically all the engine parts were furnished by Albert, whose father and uncle operated a small dairy farm. I was often a bit curious as to the source of some of those choice mechanical necessities, but as long as I was confident that their farm machinery was still operating, I ceased to worry.

As soon as the parts were assembled, we connected a small container of gasoline to the carburetor, put a teaspoonful of gasoline and a little oil in each cylinder, then replaced the spark plugs. Then came the moment of truth! Was everything in place, and all connections steadfast?

The starting job was assigned to Albert, who, with an air of dignity, assumed the role assiduously and started cranking. The old engine gave a few puffs, but refused to start. My prayers were answered when the magneto plug was removed, cleaned and replaced. The engine fired and continued to run. With no muffler, the motor was so loud that we could hardly hear our own shouts of joy! The roar of the machine brought our parents and the neighbors as well!

With Easter vacation coming up we felt that some progress could be made in locating more components for our car, but there were other matters that took precedence over the construction of our "kid made" jalopy. The yards and walks needed to be raked and cleaned, the garden spaded up and raked off, after having a liberal dose of bovine fertilizer applied, and a general sprucing up of the estate was in order.

The garden rewarded us with a generous supply of angleworms, which we kept in a large pail of soil and wet leaves, for when the trout season opened. We also helped Dad with converting an old outbuilding to a Taxidermy Shop, which he would be utilizing in the near future.

There were several instances during the summer when a hobo would stop by to work for a meal, and then continue on from one place to another. One vagabond who came to town each summer to visit relatives, would relate his experiences in various parts of the country. He would hitch-hike, ride the rails, or just walk. In winter, the fellow would manage to be in an area of warmth and sunshine, mingling with others of his kind at particular locations. He would leave with a couple of dollars in his pocket and return with nothing less. He always appeared trim and healthy.

We kids were infatuated with the colorful descriptions of places that to us, seemingly existed only in an imaginary world. We'd make mental notes of certain strange, yet incredible places, but time caused them to drift silently away like clouds in the sky.

During summer, the tourist business began to improve to the point that Dad, along with Hazel's father, added an ell to one side of the house. Within that 20-foot-square structure appeared a soda fountain, ice cream cabinet with four-flavor tubs, glass shelves to support soda glasses and banana-split dishes, and a large mirror behind the fixture. There were some wire frame tables and chairs, along with a wicker lounge sofa and chairs. Besides the front door, flanked by two large windows, a pair of French doors provided access from the main dining room.

This addition to the business was an advantageous one, since it provided an added attraction for patronizing tourists. The theoretical fly-in-the-ointment with this operation was the apparent lack of personnel. However, I'm sure that our elders had foreseen a solution to the problem in the form of a fourteen-year-old soda jerk and his younger brother. I could almost hear their clandestine remarks, "Just something to give them some responsibility." Then, perhaps, "At least we'll know where they are, and what they're up to, part of the time!"

My brother and I predicted that it could be fun making ice cream sundaes, soda drinks and packing containers full of ice cream. Of course Dad, the conservative one, made it very clear that we were not to sample the merchandise! There would be suitable times and circumstances governing that privilege.

The soda fountain soom became operational. We stocked four flavors of ice cream, chocolate syrup, fruit toppings and nuts, along with Coca-Cola syrup. Carbonated water, for ice cream sodas and Coca-Cola drinks, was piped to the fountain from a cask in the basement of the house. The cask, fitted with rockers, needed to be agitated from time to time to restore pressure. There was much to learn that was new and exciting.

Ice cream cones took regular or large scoops, dependent upon the customer's selection. Regular size cost a nickel; large, a dime. The bulk ice cream was packed in cylindrical pint or quart cardboard boxes with covers, watched carefully by the customer, to make sure they were completely filled. Repeat customers soon gave up watching, for no one was ever given less than ordered—sometimes more!

As summer progressed, Junior and I took turns at the ice cream parlor. At times, Hazel would take over (when a major cleaning job was in order), allowing my brother and I to go fishing, swimming, play ball, or get together with friends for a corn roast, or overnight camping. I still had my lawn mowing job and I always enjoyed an evening of trout fishing with artificial flies.

Brother Bobbie was still too young to get involved in some of our group activities, but we tried entertaining him as often as possible. In another ten or twelve years, he would be experiencing some of the more exciting seasonable thrills of hunting, fishing and participating in the joys of nature, as Junior and I had heretofore, and continued to value and appreciate in later years.

# Chapter 10

My first year of high school was a new adventure, riding a bus ten miles to and from school and meeting new friends picked up along the way. Loren, the driver, was an easy-going individual who was compatible with his charges. Whenever someone misbehaved, that person got an icy stare from the rear-view mirror and a word of caution. If the annoyance continued, the bus was halted at the edge of the highway and the instigator invited to leave. That was most effective, and the dispute ended.

After having been accustomed to a class of seven or eight in the elementary school, it seemed both confusing and exciting to be involved with thirty or more in one class! Engaging in various subjects in their corresponding rooms, with separate teachers, was a venture unlike any previous in my educational process. Junior would be getting an abundance of valuable information before his freshman indoctrination next year!

With autumn came the annual transformation of nature from the monotonous green of summer, to its colorful celebration of fall. Our feelings were mixed with the wonder of nature and the sadness and despairing thoughts of the bleak, leafless skeletons to be. But then we, the bold and resolute, adjusted to the impending change of seasons.

Dad's taxidermy shop was in full operation, in preparation for the deer and bear season and, hopefully, the many trophies to be mounted. People who are not familiar with the process describe the art of taxidermy as a "stuffing" of animals, birds or fish. The word stuffing refers to padding in a cushion or furniture, or preparing a fowl for roasting, *not* the art of taxidermy!

Working along with my father (mostly offensive chores), I learned that each trophy was carefully skinned and the body used as a model for a built-up replica. Deer and bear heads were skinned and the skulls used as a framework for the finished product. Preparation of the boney apparitions is where I came in!

My first job was removing all of the flesh possible from the skull, then boiling the remainder until loose. The boiling pro-

cess was done in an outer shed, due to the offensive odor—
which I hope that I never have to inhale again! I would usually
boil two or three at a time, removing the loosened tissue, re-
peating until the skull was clean.

This was supposed to be a "recreational" segment in my
life's much varied educational program and though unpleasant,
I never regretted having followed it through. My dad was a
good teacher, furthering my interest in completing several of
the finished mounts. As I became somewhat involved in this
work, I often wondered how many other youngsters got the
opportunity to delve into a rare and diverse part of learning
such as this! I was also curious as to how may more of these
seemingly remote occupations I would be exposed to in the
years to come.

With all of his work, Dad always found time for "his boys."
He was as delighted as we, when hunting season opened in the
fall and fishing season began in the spring, for then the three
of us would enjoy outings together. Bobbie would become a part
of it in the future.

In deer hunting, where we were familiar with the area,
Junior and I were allowed to "play dog." We were still weapon-
less, but we enjoyed every minute of it.

Dad and two or three other hunters would take stands in
likely deer runways across a mountainside or on the crests of
ridges. Junior and I would give them a certain allotted time to
get in place (I always carried a watch and compass) before we
started our "drive." We positioned ourselves in a lower section,
parallel to the watchers, and about a hundred yards from each
other. After checking my compass, I would let out a howl and
proceed slowly toward the hunters, which could be a half-mile
or more. Keeping our spacing abreast of each other was no
problem, with our barks and howls providing guidance.

We were constantly aware of our surroundings which, at
times, rewarded us with the glimpse of a curious deer that
paused momentarily to determine the cause of the impertinent
ruckus. If we "jumped" a deer, we would let each other know
and be on the lookout for others. The buck deer, through experience with this agitation before, left the real estate pronto! He
seldom stopped until a safe distance away, but sometimes was
interrupted in lofty flight by a well-placed bullet. More often
though, he would disappear like a four-legged phantom. No
trophies were taken on this hunt, as the deer were all does.

There were occasions when inexperienced hunters from

outer municipal areas, lodging at our tourist home, would require Dad's services as a guide. Most were conciliatory in nature and respected Dad's felicitous attitude toward firearm safety, the use of proper equipment, and adherence to regulations. There were instances, however, that tried his patience, and caused him to wonder if it was worth the endeavor.

One group of three weekend "boarders," equipped and dressed as seasoned hunters, drove Dad to distraction for two days. He would take them up the side of a mountain, place them in strategic spots, return to the starting point in a roundabout way, then flail the brush back to the watchers. There had been deer signs, but none came out to be seen.

On the next day, using the same system, Dad herded a buck that must have possessed suicidal tendencies out to one of the neophytes. The guy shot several rounds, turning the animal back down the hill toward Dad, who, believing the deer to be wounded, downed it with one well-placed shot. We determined later, that the deer had but one bullet hole.

When the group reassembled at the eight-point deer carcass, Dad instructed the shooter to field dress the animal before dragging it out to the car. The fellows looked at each other with expressions of apprehension and terror, for they had no inkling of the process. As far as they were concerned, the guts went with the animal!

Dad rolled up his sleeves and went to work. He first slit the animal down the belly to open the innards cavity. The shooter, without hesitation, began vomiting all over the place, with his buddies turning ashen as well. After the steaming mess was pushed aside to provide sustenance for coyotes, foxes and bobcats, a rope was tied around the antlers and the carcass dragged out to the car.

Back at the house, the deer was hung up for the night. During the evening, the fellows asked for some information on butchering the animal when they returned to the city. Dad was still a little strung out from the day's work and put them off until morning when they were to leave. Perhaps his irritation would subside by then.

When morning came, they paid the lodging bill, and proceeded to get Dad to help them load the deer on their car. At that time, one of them asked Dad how much they owed him for guiding. Dad, being as conservative as possible, mentioned that twenty dollars would do. At that, the three got into a huddle, then one emerged and stated, "We'll give you ten."

Then another stepped forward and mentioned that they still hadn't found out how to butcher the deer.

The adrenalin burst into Dad's veins and expletives erupted from his clenched teeth, as he bodily loaded the deer carcass, unaided, onto their auto. As he did so, he announced with austerity, "As far as I'm concerned, you can all dine on the whole thing, hair, hide and hoofs." He added that it would be a cold day in that hot place, before he would lower his dignity to their level again! After they left, Hazel, in her gentle, sympathetic manner, declared, "I should have charged them more on the lodging."

This encounter was the exception. Most clients were cautious, used good judgment and respectfully appreciated the untiring efforts that Dad put forth in their behalf. During the latter part of the deer and bear hunting season, it was not uncommon to scare up a black bear that was filling up on beechnuts or acorns. It was near hibernating time and they needed the extra fat to keep them through the winter.

Many of the beasts were shot by deer hunters, principally for their hides, which were made into rugs. Most had the finished head attached with the mouth open displaying those large, white teeth. The long impressive claws protruding from the paws were a deterrent to any adversary.

A dedicated sportsman would not shoot a sow bear with cubs. Those little balls of fur need the warmth and nourishment of the mother for one season only. The next year they would be out on their own, and mom would be having one or two more little darlings while in hibernation—provided she doesn't wind up as a rug in front of a fireplace!

With Dad's guiding and playing host to the patronizing public, an accumulation of taxidermy work had appeared at the shop. Junior and I pitched in to help in any way we could, whenever we had spare time. School work was most important, according to our elders, with other tasks secondary. I had been relieved of the skull boiling and was helping with some of the forming. Dad was the artist with plaster and finished off some of the rough basic work. Guess who had my boiling job? Yep, Junior, of course!

In addition to the regular taxidermy work, there was an abundance of deer and bear hides to be salted, packed, and shipped to a tannery downstate. Upon their return, they were finished according to the order, with Hazel doing the sewing of the scalloped border on the bear skins. Dad was ready with the bear head implants, complete with the big brown glass eyes, and that Ipana smile!

It wasn't "all work and no play," but with the business being only seasonal, it was imperative that the family utilize its resources to prepare for the slower intervals. Winter was a fairly dormant period for tourists. Other than some shop work everything was slowing down, except for the wood and coal consumption in the every-hungry furnace. Fortunately we had stocked a good supply of fuel during the fall.

Once in a while we would set up the Lionel electric train that Santa brought us a few years back, just to get Bobby squealing with joy. Then there were the radio programs that everyone enjoyed on our new, big Atwater Kent, with the large speaker that sat majestically on top.

Every two weeks or so, whenever we felt that we could afford it, we all piled into Dad's old 1932 Buick and attended a movie at the Palace Theater in Lake Placid. It was usually a musical that the whole family enjoyed, and kept us kids dreaming until the next one came along.

Then, in winter, there was always the snow to play in and ice to skate on for the youngsters. Of course, Junior and I, along with others in the community, had evolved into more daring adventures without much restraint. This winter would be just a continuation of the last one!

This year, we were going to try to consider our elder's feelings and, if possible, tone down the escapades to a reasonable level.

# Chapter 11

Before a highway was completed to the summit of the 4,800-foot-plus Whiteface Mountain, we hiked to the top via a well-worn trail, pausing now and then for a drink from numerous cold springs. Spellbound, we gazed across lesser peaks to sparkling Lake Placid with its three islands, Hawk, Moose, and Buck.

Some time later, Buck Island was to be a summer home of the renowned vocalist, Kate Smith, whom I met on the lake while I was trolling for those big rainbow and lake trout. I can still see her cruising along in her *Sunshine II*, kerchief blowing in the breeze, smiling and waving.

I remember how thrilled I became, catching a glimpse of then Governor Franklin D. Roosevelt, as he turned a shovel of soil at the ground-breaking ceremony for the start of the new Whiteface Mountain Memorial Highway in Wilmington, New York. Although I was only ten years old, I was impressed by his courage in the face of his handicap of paralysis, and admired him greatly.

When he was overwhelmingly elected President of the United States, I felt proud that I had been in his presence at an earlier time. I have always been thankful to Dad for taking us to view that historical moment.

After President Roosevelt took office, a vision of hope prevailed. Our small town had not been as abruptly affected by the financial debacle of 1929 as the large cities. Its influence came slowly, indirectly, and in time, positively. It was an inconvenience we learned to live with.

The first year of the new President's term produced unprecedented legislative activity covering a multitude of programs to stimulate the economy. A huge public works program would give people a variety of employment opportunities, boosting morale and faith in the future. An air of confidence and anticipation became evident everywhere.

In our particular area, the Civilian Conservation Corps (CCC) was very active. Small settlements of barrack-type living quarters were erected in various locations and hundreds of men worked on many projects. Trails were cut from access roads to distant lakes, ponds, and points of interest throughout the countryside. Lean-tos were built at favorable locations along these trails for the use of campers and hikers.

These projects gave employment to persons from all walks of life and provided gratifying results as well as generous compensation. The completed projects were developments, planned for the prosperity to come when vacationers would flock to the wilderness, providing a source of income for local businesses.

As the immediate effect of the depression came slowly to the rural communities, so did the recovery. We began to notice improvements quite some time after the noted general recovery was evident in metropolitan areas.

Figuratively speaking, the tourist business would be dependent upon people with fat wallets, in need of rest and relaxation. In order for that to come about, the individual needed to be gainfully employed for a definite length of time before he could line our pockets with cash. That, of course, boiled down to finite inactivity!

We planned to use our resources in to enlarge our facilities. We had consolidated our living arrangements to conserve space, heat and electricity. Junior and I had been sharing a room off the kitchen with a partition separating Grandmother's sleeping quarters from ours, closing up most of the guest rooms.

The dining area had been partitioned off to half its original size, and the ice cream parlor closed for the winter. Uncle Les had taken off for greener pastures the year before, cutting the number of residents to six. Our faithful canine, Sport, had his own little palace in a sheltered corner of the backyard, which he valiantly defended against invaders. We often took him into the woods to chase rabbits, but he was always ready to come home when we were.

Our expansion plans were based on our projected needs for the expected influx of clientele that had sampled our hospitality in the pre-depression years and had expressed their interest to return.

One change that Junior and I looked forward to was having our own room. I had just turned fifteen in early December and was in my second year of high school. Junior would be fourteen in late March and in high school the next fall, making it imperative that we have our own private room. I also kept reminding myself that, one more birthday and I could be the eager recipient of those licenses where I would be legally qualified to drive, to carry a rifle and perhaps do some fur trapping! I had already been studying Lynch's book on successfully outwitting the fur-bearers, and a booklet on bait and scent formulas. The latter had not been mentioned to the elders, for obvious reasons!

Junior and I got right to work on our room on the second floor, next to Dad and Hazel's. The room had been closed up since last fall, which made some cleaning, painting of walls and trim, and a fresh coat of paint on the wood floor necessary. Hazel and Grandmother made us some curtains for the two windows, found some scatter rugs, and now, with the twin beds, dresser, drawer chests, chairs and lamps, we were in seventh heaven!

Dad was generous with his praise for our work, and after some pats on our backs and an announcement of his pride to the others, he mentioned that there were six more bedrooms to go! Oh well, we had time on the weekends, and Dad had been good to us! So we let the matter rest.

Our weekends at home were never complete without attending church on Sunday morning, with Grandmother protesting any activity that involved work on the Sabbath. She gradually became acclimated to the recreation involving hunting and fishing, however, as long as it was accomplished in the afternoon. We even got to do some work, as long as it didn't make noise! She stuck to her own rules, regardless. Other than the necessary cooking, she spent her day reading, writing letters, or exercising her favorite rocking chair.

When weather permitted, we were out skating, skiing, or sliding with friends. Lake Placid was only fifteen miles away and Dad would often take a few of us over there for skating in the Olympic Arena when no exhibitions were scheduled. There could be up to fifty or more skaters on the ice at one time, and everyone skated in the same direction, around and around the outer rim. Figure skating enthusiasts used the center area. Anyone skating in the opposite direction was not only reprimanded, but often knocked down and out!

When driving up the main street to the arena, we passed the regulation speedskating oval in front of the high school, where records were set during the 1932 Olympic Games. It was here that Jack Shea, a native of Lake Placid, broke the speedskating records in two events, taking two gold medals.

What always caught my eye as we passed this area was a small ski jump at the upper right side of the school building.

Apparently this was used by amateur ski jumpers as a prelude to an Olympic sized one later on. I figured that if those youngsters could make a go of it, then why couldn't I? After all, hadn't I been successful on our home-made jump?

My teasing paid off when Dad, figuring that I would back out, finally agreed. Grandmother and Hazel both protested, but the die was cast! On the next sunny Saturday we took some friends to skate. Dad smiled as he tied my skis on the car top, still believing that later I would regret not bringing my skates. I would show them, I thought. Just wait and see!

Carrying my skis on my shoulder, as professionals do, I reached the base of the sloped landing, noticing that it appeared much higher than from the street—and steeper too! However, as I stared up at the chute, a young fellow came sailing off the ramp, as gracefully as an eagle, and landed halfway down the hill. When I finally struggled up the stairs to the platform, another jumper, smaller than the first, took off and was out of sight in a few seconds.

"Holy mackerel! This is a lot higher than it's supposed to be," I stammered loudly, and a jumper behind me laughed. As I looked down to where Dad and the boys stood watching, they appeared a lot smaller in size. I began to have second thoughts about this caper! What alternatives did I have now? I could walk back with a defeated and shameful countenance, or I could disappear over the hill and never come back, or . . . ?

"What's the matter, gonna chicken out? Or you gonna stand there with your mouth open?" That's when I thought, so what? This is an amateur's jump, and I'm an amateur! I didn't push off for extra speed, as was standard procedure. I just let myself go. It seemed as if I was doing a hundred miles an hour when I left the chute, with no lift, soared like a vulture and landed like a dodo bird, tumbling down the slope, minus my skis. Other than a twisted knee, a sore shoulder and fractured vanity, I was in pretty good shape.

As I returned to the street, the only comments I heard were, "Hey, you're still alive!" I presume that was consolation for having tried. My excuse was that I just needed more practice, but deep down I was fairly sure that I wouldn't attempt that again! Well, not right away.

# Chapter 12

With spring came hopes for a new and profitable season for the tourist business, one that would carry on for years in the future. We didn't realize it now, but in just a few years we would be at war! Although our country would prosper, all effects would be channeled to the conflict effort. The tourist business, as well as individuals, would be a victim of the belt-tightening sacrifices. But now, these ugly aberrations were far from our minds. The confidence prevalent throughout the country could even be felt in our little corner of the universe!

After the fishing season was under way, Junior and I had introduced ourselves to some delicious cold-water brown trout, which were prepared by Grandmother's special process, and eagerly devoured by all.

One of our repeat clients, who was a representative of one of the major fishing tackle companies, checked in with his wife and daughter on this trip. The daughter, about three years older than I, was beautiful, friendly and very charming. Junior and I were stumbling over each other to get close, and when talking, the words we uttered were indistinct mumbles. However, before she left, we were conversing more sensibly about our mutual interests and plans for the future. I apologized for our barbaric behavior, but she shrugged it off and said that she understood. Oh, what a gal! Why couldn't I have been older!

Grandmother played an important role in the success of the tourist trade, not only by her delicious food preparations, but with her colorful and descriptive tales of long ago. Many of her exciting narratives were repeats and often to the same person or group, but out of respect, they never acknowledged their awareness.

It was evident that Dad had inherited this trait, since he would join a group of guests on the front porch in the evening and relate exciting tales from the past. He specialized in real life stories that involved the "rum runners" of the 1920's, portrayed in such a manner, one would almost seem to be a part of the action. With prohibition in force, there was big money in smuggling whiskey from Canada to illegal distributors in the U.S. Being close to the border, we experienced a number of chases involving smugglers and police.

Most of this exciting adventure was before my time, but in my very early years, I can remember being awakened by the sound of high-speed automobiles racing ahead of the troopers down our main street. From our parents' bedroom we had a "ring-side seat" to the route, which passed the house, made a sharp turn to the left, and across an old iron bridge, southbound. These races, in retrospect, were not unlike the antics portrayed in the old cops-and-robbers movies! The cars were usually open touring sedans, with souped-up engines that really roared!

One race that I vividly remember suddenly came to a halt when a smuggler's auto didn't make the corner and wedged between the bridge's main beam and the sidewalk railing. The two occupants wound up in our dining room in the company of two troopers and the doctor who had the messy job of stitching up their cuts. We never did hear what became of the whiskey, but presume that it found a safe haven nearby.

With the approach of summer, my brother and I began thinking about where we left off with our auto building project. In the meantime, Dad had investigated a rumor that someone had a Model-T Ford touring car in need of a motor. It didn't take a lot of figuring to come up with one of two solutions to the dilemma. Either we sell the engine to the owner of the car, or we buy the car in which we put our engine. The latter sounded more interesting to us, but we would have to scrape up the cash to make the deal a reality.

The car owner wanted a hundred dollars for the bucket of bolts, but Dad offered sixty. Now the "horsetrading" began. It went to ninety-seventy, and then it was ours for seventy-five dollars, which Dad would bring when we towed the car home. He knew that once we had the monster assembled and purring like a kitten, it should be worth a hundred fifty, at least! That's a 100 percent profit—Dad's kind of figuring!

Other than installing the engine, we moved the fuel tank from under the seat to an elevated area behind the dash board. The Model T didn't have a fuel pump, so was gravity fed to the carburetor. This meant that one would need to go up a steep hill in reverse, consequently the change of the fuel tank location.

We ran the auto around the backyard, but that wasn't good enough. None of us had drivers' licenses yet, nor a registration plate for the car. However, for Dad to check out his investment, he agreed to tow us (with engine running) about a half-mile up the highway to a flat area on a plateau off the main road. There we had about a mile on an old logging road on which we could "open her up."

Dad took us for a spin first, to check out the brakes, transmission and whatever. With the Model T, there were three pedals—forward on the left, reverse in the center and brake on the right. On the steering wheel shaft were the spark lever on one side, and the accelerator lever on the opposite side. The former needed to be up while cranking, to prevent a kick-back that could break one's arm!

The clutch pedal, when pushed all the way down, gave low gear. As the car got under motion, the pedal was released all of the way up to be in high gear. Neutral was half way in between the low and high, and the emergency brake was a must!

As far as speed was concerned, with the four of us proudly sharing the seating, we estimated the speed at about thirty-five miles per hour, wide open. The speedometer didn't work, but it was fast enough to make our hair blow in the breeze! We had triumphed in our achievement, and were joyful with the outcome. We could readily see that Dad was proud also as he towed us home, where we put the "old girl" to rest for the time being.

That seemed to be the summer of the camping craze. For various reasons, people were coming out of their doldrums and into nature's domain. There was also a new public consciousness from past experience, that had taught frugality. Camping out may have been less comfortable, but for the more thrifty, it was an economical outlet for the desire to get away from it all. Both private and public campsites were appearing in advantageous areas, providing sites for those having large tents or trailers. Water, electricity, bathrooms (of one type or another) and other facilities became more available as the trend continued.

For those who backpacked with supplies and light tents to the lakes, ponds and mountain lookouts, the trails and lean-tos built by the CCC would prove to be a welcomed benefit.

With the drift toward "roughing it," the tourist trade was limited to the comfort-prone well-to-do, or elderly persons, who just needed relaxation. The restaurant would pick up additional business from travelers passing through, some staying overnight. Then there was the ice cream parlor, which would do well, both from local people and those camping out.

Junior had taken over my lawn mowing jobs, while I spent more time dishing out ice cream, sundaes and sodas. I took some time out once in a while to do some fly fishing, especially in the evening, when trout were rising.

My favorite area for fly fishing was in the shallows, upstream from our early-season fishing spot that I mentioned in the very beginning of this narrative. The larger trout, usually found in the pools below, would work up into the shallower water in early evening and lurk under overhanging foliage near the banks.

I released practically all the fish that I caught, unless one was extra large. The early-season cold water trout were much tastier than those caught in the warmer water of summer. Some rainbow trout had been introduced in an experimental stocking program and, although they were much smaller than the browns at first, they were hardy and spunky fighters. I enjoyed catching them on a small wet fly, playing them and then letting them go to grow.

Over the summer, I probably caught and released the same fish several times. Had I kept them, there would have been less to catch later, and less for our paying fishermen, who brought business to our area and were happy to do so. They just kept on coming back! Both the east and west branches of the AuSable River were noted in several fishing journals and in sporting magazines as some of the most productive trout streams in the northeast. They had also been favored in producing a number of record fish. I was proud to be a part of it!

Summer was also time to make preparations for winter, to harvest wild berries, as well as garden produce. Grandmother preserved all of the berries we could pick, which, to us kids was a miserable job, but we did it anyway because we knew how important it was to us all.

Mid-week was the best time for our family to get away, when the tourist business was not as brisk, so Hazel and Bobbie stayed put and the remaining four of us headed for the bush. The first berries, and the worst to pick, were the wild strawberries. They were so small and well-hidden under grass and leaves that it was a back-breaking job.

A few weeks later, it was the raspberries that were becoming ripe and ready for picking. These were not as tiring as the strawberries, for one could pick them at a crouch or a back-spraining half-bend! A blueberry patch would produce many pails of delicious berries, when they could be stripped from the bushes by the handful. Of course the discomfort here was that your knees would get sore! There were plains blueberries and mountain blueberries, and there was supposed to be a difference, but I have yet to discover it!

Now with blackberries, the last of the summer season, you'd find that you could stand erect among the head-high plants and pick to the heart's content. The only catch here, was that you had to wear a suit of armor to defend yourself from the sharp briers, just aching to draw blood! Black bears gorge themselves on blackberries to give themselves extra fat for hibernation.

One large blackberry patch I found while wandering through a different area, had extra large and luscious fruit hanging from tall, thick, formidable looking bushes. Here, I thought, I could fill my big pail in short order! That was the biggest patch I had ever seen! As soon as I had filled my pail, I'd go and get the others to come over to my bonanza!

When I started into the briars, tasting a few morsels as I went, there was a rustling noise at the other end of the patch. Oh, no, I thought, someone else had found it too! Then I yelled, "Who's there?" I didn't get an answer, but a half-grown bear stood up and faced me. We were only a few yards apart, staring at each other for a long two seconds, before taking off in opposite directions!

I concluded that bear would do his gorging at night from now on, and I would do my berry picking elsewhere!

# Chapter 13

In late August 1935, at age fifteen, I had been noticing muscle aches and numbness in the lower back and leg tendons. When it was diagnosed as poliomyelitis, I was scared out of my wits. It was learned that I had to be isolated for my protection, and for the safety of others.

I was moved to an apartment over our garage, with Grandmother as my sole companion. I laid flat on my back on her wallpapering board for the first week, then was allowed to use a hard mattress, still lying on my back. During all this time, I was on a diet of dairy products and foods high in calcium.

My grandmother stayed with me at night, and checked in on me at short intervals during the day, keeping hot packs available and fruit drinks within reach. Without her diligent and caring attention, there might have been serious consequences. I loved my grandmother very much and it was not difficult to understand that the feeling was mutual.

Missing the start of my second year in high school didn't bother me as much as missing out on those autumn jaunts in the woods, that I enjoyed so fully. Perhaps this obsession was a catalyst in producing my will to survive and fight back! My mind was working overtime to devise a method of restoring normalcy to my weak muscles.

On the doctor's next visit, I practically begged him to let me up onto my feet! He chuckled, and after checking my reflexes, set up a regimen for exercise while lying down. I must have smiled widely at the encouraging news, for he shook his finger at me and warned me not to try anything foolish!

In a couple of days, I was on my wobbly legs, with no pain or numbness—just weakness. It seemed as if I had been reborn! Within the next few days, the infection had left, and I was able to join the family that I hadn't hugged in nearly four weeks!

During my confinement, Grandmother mentioned that two other young individuals, some distance away, were enduring the same disorder. We learned sometime later that one survived with partial paralysis, while the other case was terminal. We all—including Dr. Culver—agreed that I was fortunate.

My school chums were happy to have me back, but were

over-protective at first. I understood their feelings, but assured them that I was fine. I had some school work to catch up on, which would keep my evenings busy for awhile. Though my legs were still a bit shaky, walking to my classes and up and down stairways helped in a therapeutic way.

Helping Dad in the shop subdued my anxieties regarding our annual fall outings. His assurance that everything would work out as planned inspired the confidence that I couldn't muster alone. He was the type of individual who could always solve our problems. If something seemed difficult or insurmountable, he had an alternative.

To bolster my spirits, the following Saturday Dad took Junior and I for a ride on some old back roads to look for deer signs. Having an inkling as to where the four-legged creatures were hanging out would be valuable information to have in our noggins when the deer season opened in a few weeks. I was still unable to obtain a hunting license until early December, which would be too late for the big game season. However, I could do some small game hunting for grouse, and get Sport out for rabbit hunting. That hound loved the woods!

Christmas placed second on my want list, for at sixteen I could get my driving permit, my combination hunting and fishing license as well as a trapping permit. My sights were set for the long range!

I planned on trapping foxes and mink during the winter, and in the spring and fall, raccoons, skunks and muskrats. I had prepared some fox bait during the summer, using chicken innards and some secret ingredients recommended by Mr. Lynch.

Some of this obnoxious matter was buried in glass jars beneath a corner of Grandmother's garden. We needed to use caution when the soil was spaded up next spring. Should one of the jars accidentally been broken, the contents would have stunk up the whole unsuspecting neighborhood!

Before deer season opened, we did some road-hunting for grouse. Beside those back woods roads that we had travelled recently, were old stone walls, brushy spots, and open areas. Ruffed grouse, which we called partridge, were partial to that type of environment. They would feed in or along the roadsides, or perch on the stone walls where, if alarmed, they would simply hop down the back of the wall into the brush. Some would fly up into the sanctuary of the trees, but this usually was a costly mistake on their part, as they were easy targets for the shotgun.

In the not-too-distant future we would also be hunting pheasants and woodcock with one of Dad's hunting companions and his pointer, Belle. This sport required a rapid response to a flushed bird as it takes off in a flutter of wings for an unknown destination. If you happen to be fortunate in spotting where the bird disappeared, it was possible that the dog would point it again, possibly in the company of others. An experienced and well-trained pointer or setter is a must for successful and enjoyable bird hunts.

In preparing for the expected influx of deer trophy mounts, Dad had made plaster molds for use in manufacturing his own papier-mache forms. Junior and I helped laying in, brushing, overlapping, and still more brushing the thick adhesive on strips of rosin-saturated paper in the half-molds. The two halves were cemented together when dry. What a reprieve from that skull boiling job of the previous year!

Neither of us was planning on following this line of work in the future; this occupation is one that not every Tom, Dick and Harry would be interested in. Then, also, one never knows when the subject of taxidermy might surface at some important gathering, and the knowledgeable one could become the life of the party!

Most tenderfoot deer hunters prefer the early part of the season, with less severe climatic conditions. In mid-to-late October, the woods may be dry and often a fire hazard, but quite comfortable when one just prefers to sit. Unless you have a deer drive in progress, just find a likely spot near a deer trail, be quiet and, as the old-timers say, "Let the deer come to you." When others are thrashing about in the area, they could, unknowingly, put some game out to the sitter!

A couple of fellows from downstate, who were friends of friends of ours, popped in on a Friday evening for a weekend of hunting. They were seasoned outdoorsmen, but not familiar with our area, so Dad volunteered his services, as well as those of his two favorite young human hounds!

My brother and I had played dog last season in the same section selected for Saturday morning. The finger-like ridges of mixed evergreen and hardwood forest extended from a swamp to the upper reaches of a mountainside. This didn't present any problem as far as my weakness was concerned, for my strength was returning rapidly. The romping in the wilderness would provide a boost to my physical and my mental posture.

Just being out in the woods was the best medicine.

Junior and I were dropped off near the swamp while Dad and the other two left the car farther up the mountainside, then hiked to an old logging road. We allowed them time to spread out, then took our positions in the lower area, near the beginning of our planned drive.

The leaves were so dry that they sounded like corn flakes under foot. Any deer that heard us coming would get out of the area fast! We spaced ourselves about a hundred yards apart and started working slowly toward the watchers, letting out a howl or bark periodically to verify our location.

On a small rise covered with evergreens, I heard a crash, and saw three whitetails bounding up the ridge. No rifle shots followed, so I assumed they were all illegal does. I yelled to my brother, informing him, and he replied that he had seen a big deer walking through the evergreens toward the hunters stationed on the logging road above.

When we arrived at the end of our drive, we found that Dad got a look at the three does, but not the buck. The first watcher had a sheepish expression. It seems that at the time Junior and I were just starting out, the fellow had a sudden call from nature. Deciding that there was plenty of time, he leaned his rifle against a tree, stepped aside, and went on with his duty. He suddenly heard a noise in the leaves, and there stood a multi-antlered buck watching him. While trying to make the decision of grabbing his gun, or pulling up his pants, the buck took off in a different direction! I doubt that the fellow ever lived that one down! That buck really took advantage of that indecisive moment to lengthen his life span by at least one more day.

The following day, Sunday, Dad took the fellows out with some of the local hunters to another area. When they returned in the early afternoon, they filled us in on having seen deer, but none they could identify as being legal.

Most hunters native to the Adirondacks prefer the latter part of the deer season, usually near Thanksgiving time, when there is snow for tracking. That is also the time of the rut, when the bucks tend to be more infatuated with Jane Doe than the penchant for survival.

Dad was doing some hunting with a few of his companions, while my brother and I were in school during the latter part of the season, and had obtained a good supply of venison for the winter.

*The author at two years of age, displaying a snowshoe hare, not bagged with his cork gun!*

*Junior, left, and the author at an earlier time with faithful pal, Sport.*

*Dad and his boys soon after Mother's death, 1927.*

*Mother with friend—before we kids came into her life.*

*The matriarch who dispensed affection and guidance to our young lives—our resourceful grandmother.*

*The author at twelve years of age with a product of the AuSable River, summer of 1932.*

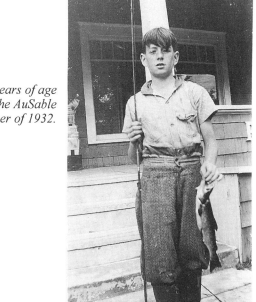

*Junior displays his angling prowess in the summer of 1932.*

*These were not a product of the AuSable, but from an Adirondack lake
—the young fisherman's dream!*

*Junior with a couple of
beauties, posing in front of our
business sign in 1932.
The AuSable River is in the
background.*

*The author posing with some of "their" taxidermy work and Junior in the foreground.*

*Left to right: Our neighbors, Don and Russ, a family friend, the author and brother, Junior, atop Whiteface Mountain, 1932.*

*Dad's mobile products business with "helpers." Left to right: Dad, Hazel, the author, Junior and Bobbie, circa 1932.*

*The author as high school baseball pitcher, 1937-38.*

# Chapter 14

I turned sixteen two days after the deer and bear season ended. Wasn't that the pits! However, I did go ahead and get my combination small game hunting license and fishing license, along with a trapping permit. My learner's permit for a driver's license was issued promptly, with caution advised on winter driving.

There was the usual amount of snow and ice which delayed my driving practice for the time being. However, it would be spring before my test would be scheduled, so Dad and I agreed that we could pick favorable times and conditions to get my practice in before then.

In the meantime, I had my sights set on some fox and mink trapping. With Dad's .22 caliber rifle under my arm, I took a couple of weekends to survey the surrounding woodlands on foot to locate signs of the fur-bearers. With the state trapping regulations requiring that the traps be visited every twenty-four hours, it would be essential to locate them in areas compatible with my after-school, evening hours. After checking out my father's inventory of traps hanging in the garage, I picked out three #2 traps for fox or bobcat, and three #1½ for mink.

These traps needed to be boiled with nut shells to remove any human scent. According to the trappers' criterion, the minute amount of oil from the shells completely neutralized the odor of steel and other foreign substances. Gloves used to handle the traps are to be odor free and kept outdoors, away from human contact. The traps that are to be placed in sets underwater, need not be deodorized, and should not be mixed with the others.

A packbasket is a must for carrying the traps, baits and scents, deodorized wire and tools. I was fortunate that Dad also had one available that had been left outdoors, free of his pipe odor. None of the trapping equipment should ever be brought indoors where it would be exposed to human odors. Just a small waft of foreign scent at the trap site will spook a fox, bobcat, marten or fisher, making them distrust that particular bait or scent in the future.

With underwater sets for mink, muskrats or other animals, one doesn't have to be as fussy about the sets, as long as the trap, chain and anchoring device are all submerged. Most trappers prefer the underwater sets which require less preparation.

I was not doing animal trapping as a profit-making business, but only as a diversion from the humdrum and monotony of the long and uneventful winter. Of course we had our outdoor sports to help us enjoy the snow and ice, and participated regularly, but this adventure bug that I was born with kept popping up! I often found it necessary to try something off the beaten track. I was fortunate that my elders understood.

As winter progressed with its arctic blasts and deep snow, it became increasingly difficult to brave the elements. By late January I had exhausted my will to continue, and reluctantly removed my traps and stored them until spring.

I had caught one large male fox and two mink, which I skinned, stretched and sold to a local fur dealer for seventy dollars. That's not much for over a month of tedious, cold, numbing work.

Until summer, school work took priority, then helping Dad in the shop. Weekends were reserved for my driving practice and for the outdoor activities of skiing, skating, sliding and hunting the snowshoe rabbit (varying hare). The latter is where our little buddy, Sport, came in portraying an authentic, high-spirited hound dog!

That mutt loved the woods more than life itself! Whenever he spied us heading for the car with a .22 rifle or shotgun, he would create a demonstration, unequalled in canine dramatics. Unhook his chain and he would be to the car in three seconds flat and playfully lap all faces that weren't covered. In the woods, however, he was all business!

I used the .22 for rabbit hunting, mainly for practice on fast moving targets. The advantage of running the snowshoe rabbit over the smaller cottontail was that the latter will usually find a secure hiding place after the first trip around, while the snowshoe will run ahead of the dog for several laps.

The sound of a baying hound, hot on the track of one of those long-legged varmints, is music to the ears of the woodsman. When Sport was out of sight and working a section of woods for rabbit scent, he used various yips, yaps, barks and whines to correspond with his efforts. If he really opened up with that deep, resonate howl, one better be alert for that white streak of fur that may be swishing by!

Sport was an intelligent and trustworthy mongrel that we considered part of the family. Most of his life was spent in the outdoors, but often, after a frigid hunt, he was allowed inside to thaw the ice from between his toes. He would lie near the kitchen stove, where one could translate his soft moans to, "Oh boy, this is the life!"

I heard, one time, about a fellow who claimed to own the most intelligent dog in the world. As the story went, when the owner selected his .22 caliber rifle from the gun rack, the dog would charge out the opened door and seek out a squirrel or opossum for his master to shoot. If the man left the house with his shotgun, the mutt would find a grouse, pheasant or rabbit. Then, as the large caliber rifle appeared, there was extra effort made to round up a deer or to tree a bear.

Then, the owner continued, a most extraordinary and incredible event came about that tended to push the canine's super intelligence! The man had repaired a friend's fishing rod some weeks before, and decided to return it prior to the opening of the fishing season. As he left the house with the rod, the dog suddenly disappeared. Puzzled as to what had excited the canine, he finally found him out in the garden, furiously digging worms!

The relentless winds of early March were chilly, but with the sun there occurred a hint of awakening. There would be another month of tempting warmth and foreboding cold, alternately straining the limits of human endurance. This discomfort, however, would soon be put to rest, as the rains challenged the remaining snow and ice, and brought out the inevitable annoyance of black flies and mosquitos.

Complaints often form a topic of conversation, which bring humans to share a common allegiance. Those who can adjust their lives to fit are truly soldiers of fortune, and have my deepest respect. In my youth, every season brought a variety of prospects for varying interests. We youngsters were those soldiers of fortune. Wherever adventure presented itself, that's where we wanted to be!

# Chapter 15

I passed my driving test on the first try and Dad was as pleased as any father could be. Of course I gave him the credit, for it was he who had provided the training.

Dad decided not to license the Model T Ford. He met some eager car buyer who made a generous offer for it that we couldn't refuse. Dad had his eye on a more up-to-date model. It was a jitney type vehicle with an enclosed cab and roofed-over truck body. Beauty was not one of its attributes, but it was a serviceable means of conveyance and in good mechanical condition. It would serve our needs, and provide trucking duties for the business as well.

Since my less than profitable days of fur trapping during the winter, I decided to make up for it the next spring by reducing the muskrat population, while fattening my wallet. Bringing in a raccoon or skunk now and then would add to the bonanza! It was still an after-school and weekend project, but having the extra daylight would be of help, especially when I could check the sets more rapidly with that machine on wheels.

I found some marshes and beaver dams beside the river only a few miles away, that were easily accessible. Other trappers were also in the area, but with the constant rise and fall of the water level, they were finding it difficult to maintain their sets at a consistent and productive depth. With this problem in mind, I began to explore possible solutions. Why not have the sets float on the surface so that they would always be on top, rather than a foot or more under?

I used two-foot lengths of old eight or ten-inch wide lumber, and nailed a shorter piece at each end, leaving room in the center to recess a small trap. The trap chain was secured underneath with staples, and used a wire of the length required to secure the board to a bush or anchor of some sort, fastened to one end. At the top of that end I drove a finish nail part way in, allowing it to protrude enough to impale a piece of carrot or an apple as a lure. My theory was that a muskrat would climb onto the board to obtain the bait, step on the trap, then dive off the float and drown.

The following Saturday I experimented with three or four

of the boards at a beaver dam that was easily accessible. I checked them on Sunday, and "eureka," the theory had worked! I then began using them in other locations, with equally good results. It wasn't long, however, before others began using the same system. After all, how can you keep anything that successful a secret?

In some of my trapping areas I found signs of raccoons, and where there were farms there were skunks which farmers were eager to get rid of. The skunk fur was the most valuable because few trappers wanted to deal with the odor. Their shield of defense was not only offensive to humans, but to other animals as well. When dispatching one, I usually kept a safe distance away, then picked up the animal, trap and all, anchoring it in the nearest stream of water, where I would retrieve it the following day. Most of the scent had been washed out of the fur by then.

I did most of the skinning and stretching in Dad's shop, but when I showed up with a skunk, it was outdoors for both him and me! Even though the animal had little odor, and didn't appear to be offensive, it was just the psychological aspect, I presumed.

I remember leaving a washed wool shirt on the clothesline for a week after having a whiff of that potent fragrance caught in its threads. Believing that it was surely descented by this time, I confidently wore it to school. Someone in my first class, who possessed super-sensitive nostrils, complained about a skunk being outside. Of course others soon followed suit. The teacher raised one of the windows, peered outside, saw nothing and gave some far-fetched excuse. The odd part, though, was that the smell remained regardless of the window position! I was pleased when that class was finished, and I could change to a sweatshirt that I kept in my locker!

My pelts were shipped to Sears Fur Marketing Service, where one could be paid extra for taking special care in preparing the pelts and stretching and drying them. My compensation was the result of unconventional and tiresome work, but with efforts that were put forth willingly.

The heretofore tranquil waters of the AuSable River were again taking their seasonal vengeance against any impediment that delayed the roiled surge to its ultimate destination. Then, in its usual conciliatory manner, it innocently portrayed the docile harbinger of Spring. Everyone in the area was conscious of its fickle conduct, and took it for granted.

It is a common adage that, "In spring, a young man's fancy turns to—love." In many cases, it could be true, when the whole world seems to explode into an array of warm breezes and sweetness. Of course, those of us who found our fancies turning to fishing or automobiles, in our pre-teen years, were now beginning to understand the true meaning of the phrase. It seemed that there should be two girls for every boy, so the possibility of having at least one for yourself would be greater!

Some of the girls that I became attracted to wound up in the arms of other fellows. However, I was alert enough to recognize the competition for popularity. I guess they were not my type anyway! I had many friends who were girls, and spent time with each of them when the opportunity presented itself.

In study hall, where the desks had side drawers, a gal would get permission to collaborate on a given subject and would come to my desk. I would pull out the drawer, pile up the contents to make her comfortable, and we would discuss life in general. After a time she would return to her desk, I would request permission to speak with someone, and be sitting on the drawer of her desk, continuing our conversation. These trivial, unplanned associations were platonic relationships between friends, and continued as such during all of my high school years.

Junior had gotten used to being called by his given name, Clayton, named after Dad, and was adapting to the latter part of his freshman year as an average student, with outside interests of fishing and hunting, of which I was also guilty. He didn't have my interest in trapping, and had to wait until the next year for his hunting license.

We were well prepared for the trout season, however, and anxious to go. We would be eagerly sampling some of those remote wilderness brooks that support native speckled trout with the golden bellies and with flesh the color of salmon. They are the most delicious trout in the world!

# Chapter 16

After a quiet winter, the business showed signs of activity once again. There would be several groups of fishermen checking in at various times during the next month eager for early trout fishing. The fly fishermen would be using fancy streamer and bucktail flies to imitate disabled minnows while the streams were still running ice water. The sophisticated fly fishing would come later in the season as the weather and streams became warmer. At that time, evening or early morning fishing was preferred.

While Grandmother and Hazel got the house and ice cream parlor in order, Dad, Junior and I did the early spring outside work of sprucing up, cleaning and painting where necessary. This coincided with our Easter school vacation, allowing us kids to sleep an extra hour in the morning, providing we didn't goof off during the day.

Getting Grandmother's garden ready for the early planting of vegetables was an essential annual occurrence, that was assigned to the "kids." We designated Bobbie, who would be six that August, to get into the act by picking up worms. He enjoyed it so much that the inevitable question arose, "When can I go fishing?" We assured him that it would be soon. I carefully spaded up the area hiding my jars of fox bait, and marked the section with a "No Planting Here" sign to protect it from cultivation. I had no idea as to when the bait would be used, but was sure that it was getting to be pretty potent material.

As a family we were indeed fortunate to be healthy, happy, and possess the ability to have survived the rigors of the past. We did not allow ourselves to be unfettered by occasional bursts of prosperity. We needed to be continually watchful, and be prepared for the down side. Credit for a successful livelihood was determined by team effort—our team.

Soon after the fishing season opened on May first, our tourist home began buzzing with activity. We all lent a hand to ease the load. Grandmother and Hazel were busy with meals, laundry, cleaning up, and general housekeeping. Dad was playing host and information center for the guests, while

Junior and I were responsible for the loose ends, when not in school. We both rode the bus to and from AuSable Forks High School, leaving evenings and weekends to help out.

After the early season rush, there came a slack period, which gave everyone a breather. There was a continued trickle of overnight guests and patrons of the restaurant and ice cream parlor, however. We anticipated a substantial boost after schools were let out for the summer, and families would be vacationing in the Adirondacks.

Our old jitney was sold and Dad bought a used 1927 Buick that was in good mechanical condition. We had to tow it home from Saranac Lake prior to getting it registered. The first problem turned out to be a reversed shift, which made high and low gears just the opposite. In towing, I lost some rubber on the road before I noticed the gear placement panel on the floor which Dad hadn't noticed either.

One Saturday afternoon, during the business lull, Junior and I packed a lunch, put our fishing gear into the back seat of the old Buick, and headed for Cascade Lakes, located in a mountainous area between Lake Placid and Keene, New York.

The ice had only recently left the two narrow lakes, nestled between steep, rocky mountainsides, offering just room enough for a two-lane highway. The lakes were positioned end to end, separated by a dam-like earthen barrier, and having a small stream as a connecting waterway.

I parked the car at a turn-out beside the upper lake, where it had reluctantly given access down the rocky slope to the water's edge. We found the water to be ice cold with a breeze to match. Worms were tried, and worms with spinners, spinners alone, and imitation small minnows, all to entice the speckled trout, but to no avail. They were just not interested.

We then moved down to the lower lake and another turn-out, where we used the same procedures as in the upper lake, in the same frigid water. However, we did catch a few small trout on spinners, which gave us enough confidence to endure the discomfort.

As it was beginning to get dark, and we were over fifteen miles from home, we decided to surrender to the elements, and head out. We soon realized that the car's lights were not working! We at least had enough sense to bring a flashlight and a few basic tools, but couldn't find the source of trouble under the hood. We felt abandoned, isolated from humanity, sitting there in the darkness, weighing the possible solutions.

56

There was little traffic on that highway at night. After several minutes, we saw headlights coming down the hill behind us. We got out of the car, which still had the hood panels up, and with our flashlight, signalled the vehicle. The young fellow looked over what he could with our dim light, and made it clear that we had to get to a lighted area.

Solving that problem would be easy, he stated. "Just follow me as closely and safely as you can, until we get down to Keene." The word "down," however, wasn't as easy as I had discerned on the trip up here. The winding hills were comparable to an Olympic ski slope and nearly as steep, and from where we stood, it might as well have been!

The fellow promised to drive slowly, making it easy to keep up by following his tail lights. Perhaps he raced cars as a hobby, for his slow speed was at least fifty miles an hour, which, augmented by the darkness, made our speed seem to be eighty, curves and all! I didn't dare slow down for fear of losing his lead, and being left back in the blackness. It was not unlike riding a bobsled run—at night. We were overjoyed and relieved to see the first street light in Keene!

We had just a very little money with us—not enough to pay a mechanic to work on the old bus, but our new friend came to the rescue again with a piece of electrical wire. He connected it directly from the battery to the headlights, and it worked! "That will get you home," he confidently said. We thanked him profusely, but he just shrugged it off with a "good luck," and left. I called home and let them know that we had some car trouble, but were on our way.

Our feeling of self-reliance was short-lived when, about a mile farther on, the lights went "poof." It was as if we had run into a solid wall of blackness. With our weak flashlight, we discovered that one of the side panels had rubbed on the wire and burned it in two. We disconnected it from the battery, twisted the wire back together and reconnected with positive results. I found a stick beside the road, which was put under the hood panel to keep the latter from touching the wire again. We were home in less than a half-hour, with a multitude of questions to be answered.

Now that we had fairly reliable transportation, as a result of Dad's repairs and meticulous mechanical checkup, we had limited access to ordinary, commonplace activities. There were rules to be adhered to, which we recognized and agreed to comply with. Among them were: No night traveling until further notice, no more trips in excess of ten miles from home, and an account of where we were going and when we expected to return. Too bad these rules were not in effect before our Cascade Lakes trip!

With school out for the summer, my brother Junior and I would be doing our annual chores of lawn work and soda fountain tending, along with keeping the yard tidy. There would be days of swimming, fishing and playing baseball, sandwiched between the "on duty" periods. We very seldom objected to disagreeable chores, like weeding the garden, since we wanted to repay in kind the thoughtful, devoted, and unselfish attention given us in the past.

The river water was beginning to warm, and with it, trout were sampling whatever hatches of flies were present. A few of the local fly fishermen would determine the new hatch by standing on the bridge over the river, catching one or two flies, and matching them with their artificial counterparts. These local fellows, who were businessmen, used the conservative approach, as did I, by releasing most of their catch for later sport. Having an abundance of fish for the paying public was good for business, and good for the future.

As to trout for eating, most people preferred the native brook trout or lake rainbow trout, the latter caught by trolling a set of small spoons with a fat night crawler behind. The naturally spawned brook trout could be found in wilderness brooks or backwoods beaver dams fed by the brooks. If the beaver dam was not over three or four years old, the brookies would be quite large and fat. Beyond that, the fish got starved out and lost their delicious taste. It was great sport catching them in a beaver dam, using artificial flies.

There were no privately-owned swimming pools in those days. Where a sandy spot in the river was found, with the water over four feet in depth—that was the swimming hole! Dad taught Junior and I to swim at a river dam a ways downstream from home, when we were four or five years old. At first, we didn't approve of his method, but it worked!

He took us, one at a time on his back, to a log bunker in the middle of the dammed river, where the water was about six feet deep. He left us there and went back to shore. We yelled for him to come and bring us back, but he pretended to ignore us. Finally, he reminded us that he had demonstrated the dog-paddle, and that we could do it just as well there as next to shore. We screamed and cried and yelled some more, but got no response.

After what seemed like an eternity, I stepped down onto a sunken log where the water was chest high, with Dad calling encouragement from the shore. I took a deep breath, pushed off, and did the fastest dog paddle on record. Then with Dad and I yelling, Junior paddled safely to shore. Years later that river dam has been washed away by ice floes, but that memory will never fade.

We had learned of a swimming hole farther up river which had rock ledges on the highway side of the water, and a wide sandy beach on the far side. Without transportation, it had been out of reach for us, until now, so with permission granted, we loaded the old Buick and took our neighbors, Don and Russ, and drove up to investigate.

It was more impressive than imagined, for just below the deep hole was a foot bridge leading across the river, aptly named "The Swinging Bridge." It served a farm located at the edge of the woods on the far side, where vehicular access was by a roundabout backwoods route from the hills. At the far end of the bridge was a path leading down to the beach area.

This became a popular attraction in the summer, providing, in addition to the beach, a series of diving shelves on the ledges, for the brave and the addled. The clear water was more than ten feet deep near the ledges and tapered to a foot or so at the beach. It was a meeting place for friends and families who abided by the unwritten rule of keeping the area clean. Whatever came in, also went out!

At times during the summer we would experience a torrential rainstorm that roiled the water and raised the level markedly. Under those conditions, for some reason, those large river brown trout would go up the tributary brooks in the high, swift current. While displaying this unorthodox behavior, they seemed to possess insatiable appetites. Using angle worms as bait, a fisherman could take his limit of up to sixteen-inch, scrappy brown trout. In every pool or eddy, there would be a giant brown lurking.

The survivors would return to the river as the flow subsided. The monster trout were seldom seen in the river. They would hide under rocks, logs, or brush along the banks during the day and come out to feed late at night. I presume this criteria is partly responsible for their size and longevity. Another example of the wonder of nature!

# Chapter 17

The first day of the hunting season fell on a school day, which eliminated my brother and I from getting out with Dad and his companions. The initiation of my first big-game license would have to wait until Saturday. In later years, new legislation by the State would allow the season to begin on a Saturday and end on a Sunday, which would allow working hunters to have the advantage of the beginning and end of the season, both being on a weekend. In the future, also having Federal holidays fall on Mondays, with a few exceptions, would provide long weekends for those who wished to pursue the recreation that filled their needs.

Now, as my brother and I were looking forward to the coming weekend, we learned that the continual dry weather had made the woodlands a veritable tinder box. With no significant rainfall for the past several weeks, and with the falling leaves creating further danger of fire, the State closed the woods as a precautionary measure. As soon as substantial rainfall made the forests safe, the season would be reopened, and extended accordingly. All hunting plans were now on hold. Those hunters scheduled to arrive during the next two weeks, had to be booked for lodging at a later date.

The news was less than favorable for the tourist business, but the delay could possibly save untold devastation. We had seen the results of forest fires, and knew the disastrous effect on the environment. As far as we were concerned, extending the hunting season was a blessing in disguise. Later in the fall there should be snow for easier tracking, and with the sometimes biting cold weather, most of the unseasoned deer hunters had reluctantly surrendered to the elements.

With no immediate rainfall predicted, Junior and I did some leaf raking around our yard and for our summer employers. We also began gathering small, frost-bitten pumpkins for our new near-miss "bombing" on Halloween night. This plan was formulated with some of our buddies to provide a surprise for out-of-town pranksters who came to our village late at night to create havoc, for which we got the blame.

Our bombing location was atop an iron bridge over the

river, which was constructed of sixteen-inch wide, flat-topped steel girders slanted upward on each end, connected by a fifty-foot girder across the top. There was a concrete sidewalk, with railing, along each side of the two-lane roadway. It was about twenty feet from the sidewalk to the top of the girder—a good height for accurate bombing, we figured. We even had our escape routes planned and rehearsed.

After dark on Halloween night, we made our final preparations. One of our group climbed up each of the slanted girders to the middle of the span, where they received the small, spongy pumpkins, carefully tossed up from the sidewalk below. After a dozen or so were stored up there, the fellows returned to wait out the appearance of our adversaries. In our ordinary mischievous pranks, we never intentionally harmed anyone, nor destroyed things and we didn't plan on it now, either. We just wanted to make the outsiders conscious of our abilities to make them unwelcome!

It was quite late and we were wondering if our out-of-towners were going to show, when suddenly, the signal came that five or six of them had just arrived and were getting out of their car some distance up the street beyond the bridge. We immediately sprang into action with two guys scrambling to the top of the bridge girders, and lying flat to avoid detection. Four of our remaining gang waited near the far end of the bridge.

When the pranksters saw us, we began with our cat-calls and derisive, aggravating insults, which set off their offensive maneuvers. As we ran across the bridge, two on each sidewalk, they were rapidly gaining on us. Then the bombardment began, with bursting pumpkins splashing them from head to toe, and causing them to fall into more of the same. They had met their Waterloo! After they finally crossed the bridge, we were nowhere in sight. We had slipped into our prearranged hiding places, and were staying there until it was safe to come out! They apparently wondered what we had in store for them next, for some of the town folk had seen them looking cautiously into every dark corner, as they retreated to their car.

We had the bridge mess to clean up the next day, but since we had a victory under our belts, we enjoyed every minute of it. It was clearly understood from this caper, that retaliation would be forthcoming any time in the future, and that trouble makers would pay dearly. For now, we were well satisfied that our strategy had worked.

Early in the second week of November, the rains came, gently at first, with a moderately warm breeze. Then, overnight, the breeze became a blustery gale that, by the next night, brought colder temperatures and a heavy, wet snow. Tree limbs were loaded and evergreens were bowing under the weight.

Plodding in the woods now would be comparable to wading the river, with snow falling, and the frigid wind biting through woolens. It made good sense to wait. In a span of two days, nature's conduct had thrust us into a decidedly different world.

This sudden transformation from fall to winter in the northern climate is an annual event that usually begins near the end of the first week in November. It often spreads the change of seasons over several days of gradually increasing adverse weather conditions, giving some warning of the winter to come. Then at other times, it is sudden and unpredictable, as demonstrated previously.

During this period, the buck deer become affected by the change in temperature and air pressure and, with the rut a prominent feature, tend to be careless. Old-time hunters speak of November 11th (Armistice Day) as the day the bucks "go wild." During this period, a learned and persistent deer hunter might meet with success in bagging his trophy by catching a buck off guard.

Unless we had some group hunting to attend to, Dad, Junior and I found "still hunting" our chief method of pursuit. We would walk as quietly as possible, keeping the wind in our faces, remembering to stop, look and listen. There have been many instances when a wise old buck would stand motionless at a safe distance, while the plodding hunter passed on by!

We often spread out at some distance apart, noting a prearranged meeting point farther ahead. This ploy often proved successful. A deer spooked by one of us would often come within the range of another.

During our extended big-game season, due to the dry woods closing, there were several inches of snow, making tracking easier, and giving us an estimate of the number of deer in a given area. Junior was tagging along with Dad, and I was some distance away using our still hunting skills as efficiently as possible. I hadn't gone far, when I came upon a fresh track of a large deer. Following the trail, I noticed the deer had veered off toward Dad's area. Then somewhere under the soft snow, my foot snapped a piece of tree limb. A short distance away, I saw that the buck had burst into high gear!

In half a minute, two rifle shots echoed from a slope of the mountainside ahead. My hunch that the shots were from Dad's .32 proved correct. When I appeared on the scene, I saw that the deer was an eight-point buck that would weigh over 170 pounds. After removing the innards, we dragged the carcass out to the car.

With the extended season winding down, and my hunting being confined to Thanksgiving vacation and weekends, Dad had me tag the deer. This would give him the opportunity to add more venison to our larder, should he get another chance. This successful hunt happened on my 17th birthday, which made the buck my gift from Mother Nature!

There would be rabbit hunting later, and I wanted to try some ice fishing with one of my school chums who had equipment. We figured that late January would find the lakes frozen solid enough to drive a car onto it safely.

In the meantime, there were preparations for the Christmas holiday, with Junior and I being assigned the task of selecting a nicely shaped tree from the nearby woods. The fresh scent of a spruce or balsam in the house seems to bring forth the awareness of this festive occasion.

That holiday season our church had a new minister who was a young lady from a city parish. She was delighted with the country, but unfamiliar with many of its indigenous qualities. Her manner allowed her to fit in well with any occasion and to appreciate a "down home" sensitivity. When she asked if some of the older boys could locate a Christmas tree for the parsonage, we gladly volunteered, and promised to seek out a special one, just for her!

We wanted to do something pleasant for her, but her naiveté kept getting in the way and enticed us to veer from our original plan. As we plodded through the evergreens to find that special tree, we happened upon a dead spruce, just the right size for a Christmas perennial. Its needles were the color of rust, and by spring, they would have fallen off to leave a once gracious evergreen but a skeleton in the forest.

"That's her tree!" Fran, the elder of our group exclaimed. We protested the decision, but the more we thought about the fun involved, the greater the appeal! The special tree was sawed off with care, for we didn't want to lose those beautiful needles, and too much vibration could ruin it.

This is where I had doubts about the caper, and wanted to

back out, but I had been a part of it from the beginning, so we set the atrocious reject from nature in the bay window. We found it necessary to tie it in place with several pieces of cord to prevent it from falling down.

When the reverend saw it, she just couldn't believe that there was such a tree anywhere. She had never, in all her life, seen anything so different, and so special! She thanked us many times before we left.

Of course we knew that the consequences were bound to happen, but after a few days with no repercussions, we began to wonder and worry. If the reverend had decorated it, that was one thing, but if there were lights put on it, there could be a fire. Fran volunteered to find out, right after church on Sunday.

However, we didn't have to wait until after the service for, although no names were mentioned in describing the caper from the pulpit, the congregation seemed to be focusing its attention on four very, very red faces!

# Chapter 18

Unless one provides himself with some means of protection from the elements, ice fishing could easily be voted the most rugged, punishing, but often rewarding pastime in the angling world. Depending upon the nature of the fish sought, there are methods to alleviate many of the discomforts, however.

I was fortunate in getting some first-hand experience with an older friend, Charlie, who had the required equipment. We were to try for northern pike or walleyed pike, using tip-ups and live minnows for bait. The latter were kept in Charlie's truck cab, to prevent freezing. The pond ice was over ten inches thick, which allowed us to have the pick-up truck close to our fishing location—henceforth, one of the comforts!

Our first job was to crank an ice auger through ten inches of the hard, frozen ice, and to dip out the chips to clear the water. The "tip-ups," which had two crosspieces shaped like an "X," also sported an upright stick with a flexible steel band attached. At the lower end of the upright, the reel holding the fishline was located. At the hook end was a short length of steel leader, which prevented the pike's sharp teeth from severing the line.

Charlie impaled a minnow on the hook and let out about twenty feet of line. Then the flexible band, having a small red flag at its tip, was hooked to the reel's tripping mechanism. When a pike grabs the minnow and swims away, it trips the device, the flag pops up, and you sprint for the hole. Sometimes the pike is still on, sometimes not!

After setting one, we warmed up in the truck (lots of hot coffee is an important prerequisite) then proceeded to install another set at some distance from the other, keeping it on a radius to the vehicle. We kept surveillance on our first set as we worked, occasionally returning to clear the ice from around the reel. We set a third tip-up and then sat in the warm truck to watch the three, clearing the ice and checking the reels at intervals.

It's a real thrill to see one of those flags pop up. Unless a northern pike is two feet long or more, it is so boney that there's not much meat. A walleye, on the other hand, is delicious eating, regardless of size above the legal limit.

When the lake or pond ice is still too thin to safely support a vehicle, the "early birds" need to bundle up like Eskimos, with hand warmers or other means of preventing frozen fingers. Then some sort of seat is necessary, having a wind shield for protection from the constant cold, arctic-like air. There isn't much to be said for comfort here!

Charlie and I caught two small (about sixteen-inch) pike, which we carefully released, and had a larger one up to the hole, before he broke loose. That one would have been a "keeper," we surmised. The saying that the big one always gets away was proving true!

The most comfortable method of fishing through the ice seems to be using an "ice shanty." These, usually home-made cubicles, vary in size from four-by-four feet or larger, to six feet or more in height, dependent upon the requirements of the fisherman. Many are built large enough to accommodate four persons on two seats, and have a window in the door and one at the other end. The unit is mounted on wooden sled-like runners, which allow it to be pushed on or off the ice. After setting it in place, and jigging holes are cut through the ice floor, water is dipped out and then poured around the runners to freeze them into place. This will keep the unit stable during high winds.

Those units are used most exclusively in jigging for the smaller fish such as yellow perch, crappies, and smelt. With a small gas or kerosene heater and ample ventilation, the little palace provides a comfortable "home away from home," oblivious to the wild outdoors. Catches are measured by the pailsfull of delicious fish. Toward spring, a watchful eye on the weather and ice is necessary to retrieve the shanties before the ice becomes too soft.

After mentioning ice fishing as a recreation pastime, I now recall having taken part in an annual late-winter project called "ice harvesting," which is all work! It was, most likely, the coldest job this side of the Arctic Circle, but a vital necessity to those who depended upon it. It was body-numbing work, but it had to be done.

About a mile out of town, there was a large pond formed years ago by damming a small brook. Below the dam was a sawmill which produced rough-sawn lumber from forest logs. The by-product, sawdust, was used to insulate the ice blocks, appropriately stored in the "ice house." While sawing and handling the foot-or-more square cakes of ice, the men using the ice tongs wore rubber trousers and aprons to keep their clothing dry. The pond produced a whole summer's supply of ice.

The cakes of ice, which were cut from the pond's surface with a large circular saw mounted on an extension arm, were subsequently loaded onto a large shallow-bed sleigh for transport to the ice house. A pile of sawdust would be waiting there, to be spread over the dirt floor of the sixteen-foot-square building. Then the first load of ice, handled by a couple of workers, was laid out on the floor in the back half of the ice house, spacing them one to two inches apart. These were then covered by the sawdust, allowing it to fill the spaces between the blocks. An additional two or three inches of sawdust was spread atop this layer in preparation for the next load of ice, which was already on its way.

This process continued for two or three days until the building was filled to capacity, and the pond completely harvested. The tally on that season's haul was estimated at over 900 cakes of ice! When blocks were removed, they were handled with ice tongs, and then hosed down to completely remove the insulating sawdust. I might add that sawdust, when dried, was also used as wall insulation in homes built during that period to make them snug and warm for the winter.

Although most families had electric refrigerators when I was in my late teens, some kept the old ice boxes for extra cold storage during the summer. When a block of ice could be purchased for a quarter, nobody seemed to mind going to the ice man's establishment, hosing down a block and bringing it home. The block would serve for three or four days, which was considerably less than the cost of using an extra electric unit.

When the subject of ice comes to mind, I remember how excited Junior and I became when Mr. Devlin came through town selling lake trout. His pick-up truck was enclosed except for a canvas curtain at the rear. When the curtain was rolled up there were "oh's and ah's" from us as our eyes feasted on those huge lake trout nestled in a bed of crushed ice. Although we knew they came out of the Great Lakes, we were dazzled by the thought of catching one of those babies in our own fishing holes! Dad would usually buy a chunk of one, which would provide a mouth-watering, baked trout dinner, along with keeping our dreams alive!

We were aware of large lake trout being present in Lake Placid, and that some were caught early in the spring, immediately following ice-out. From then on, the big ones remained in the deepest and coldest water, to be rarely hooked on large trolling spoons, worked through the seemingly bottomless pockets. To get a lure down there was a feat in itself. The line needed to be copper or lead-core, and the spoon sometimes weighted down. Pulling the lure in jerks and wobbles was a tiring process, but often a rewarding one.

Our renowned AuSable River was on its annual spring rampage, with ice floes bumping and grinding their way downstream. Then, as if a huge hand had signalled for a halt, the floes slowed and the water level rose. At some point, the slabs of ice met an obstruction and the floes began piling, wedging and crushing upon one another, causing a mammoth ice jam.

The trapped water pushed relentlessly to seek an avenue of escape, but to no avail. It had but one alternative—over the banks and around the impediment, producing a violently raging torrent, persistently pushing slabs of ice and debris to the doorsteps of surrounding residences.

While the highway department was frantically working at the jam with pike poles and dynamite, we were creating a plan for evacuating those who were in imminent danger. Being a new member of the village fire department, I was selected to evacuate an elderly lady and her dog from a residence that was being threatened by high water and ice, on the east side of the river.

From the old iron bridge spanning the ice-choked mess, I noticed that, by no means could I maneuver a boat to the front of the house, which was menaced by large blocks of ice. As I ran to the far side of the floes where an aluminum boat was available, I yelled for someone to phone the lady to meet me at the rear entrance.

The boat oars were useless in that maelstrom of raging water and ice, but by using a pike pole, I could push the ice cakes aside as I poled the boat around to my anxiously awaiting passengers. The return trip would be more difficult as we'd be fighting against the current and ice blocks. The lady was firmly gripping the boat seat, avoiding the sides as she had been instructed, while the cocker spaniel rode the bow, seemingly intent on navigation! It was a welcomed relief to get back on solid footing with all hands out of danger.

Another two hours elapsed before a channel was opened in the jam and the water began to recede, taking everything with it. The river banks were littered with grotesque forms of ice, left to melt away at its leisure. While present, it was a constant reminder of the damage and flooded basements left in its wake. It was over once again, until next year.

There were four of us upper-teenagers who had become apprentices in the village fire department. Our eagerness to perform our expected duties was often tested with some less than desirable tasks. We were to maintain an old Model T Ford fire truck, generally kept on display as an antique, rather than as a useful piece of apparatus. The veteran firemen, we presumed, gave us that responsibility to keep us from interfering with their duties, but we had other plans for that antiquated machine!

A couple of us who had had previous experience with our old Model T touring car went to work on the engine. We replaced worn parts, cleaned and checked the electrical system, and made whatever mechanical adjustments were necessary. After the motor was purring to our satisfaction, we focused our attention on the equipment. That was a disaster! What had we gotten ourselves into?

The firehose, with hydrant connections, was a jumbled mass in the hose compartment; axes, rakes, brooms, and shovels used in grass fires were rejects from who-knows-where or when! There were no boots, raincoats or helmets; it was a challenge. The veterans seemed to be amusingly indifferent to us. This lack of concern, though depressing, made us more confident that we would succeed.

Our first project was getting the vehicle stripped of its contents and then to clean it thoroughly, both inside and out. The flat lengths of firehose were connected together with a nozzle at one end and a hydrant coupling at the other. We then folded them neatly, zig-zag fashion in the hose compartment, with the hydrant connection at the outside. When fighting a fire, we would connect to a fire hydrant, leave one man at that position with the hydrant wrench, then drive speedily to the fire location. The hose would be efficiently unfolded and ready for water.

Upon demonstrating our unfaltering determination to be an effective element of the department, the older members became cooperative in furnishing us with some of their excess serviceable equipment. Until summer vacation, we would be available nights and weekends—with parents' approval, of course. We had made an impression, and were happy for it.

In late spring, whenever there happened to be a very dry

spell, there were some individuals who made a habit of burning off the dead grass on their land for the sake of enhancing the beauty and abundance of the new greenery. Nine times out of ten, the fire would get out of hand, making it necessary for the fire department's assistance to help control the blaze. Unless the fire was in reach of one of the hydrants where our old truck would be serviceable, the pumper truck, with its water storage, would be summoned. We also went along as manpower to beat the fire out with brooms and shovels.

Having had some experience in driving the Model T Ford touring car that I mentioned earlier in this narrative, I was selected as the number one operator of our pride and joy. Top speed on level roadways very seldom exceeded forty miles per hour, and on a hill, it depended on the slope. At one time, while racing to a fire up and beyond our winter sliding hill, and having the throttle wide open, a youngster passed me— riding his bicycle!

Improvements were forthcoming in that little village fire department, with more up-to-date and efficient trucks and equipment. Our old machine was retired with honors and acknowledgment of its service. For decades, it was proudly displayed as a museum piece, and in my memory it will rest as a vital part of my youth.

# Chapter 19

As summer progressed, our recreational activities became sandwiched between the responsibilities of our home, the business, and community pursuits. My brother Junior, Dad and I would take time for excursions into the wilderness, or for special events such as air shows, the county fair or a circus. When the latter was performing somewhere near, everyone attended at one time or another. Bobbie would get to attend more than once, which delighted him beyond belief!

My enthusiasm was aroused whenever an air show made an appearance at the nearest airport. I had always been fascinated by those old open cockpit biplanes, the Curtiss "Jenny," Stinsons, Wacos, and dreamt of donning helmet and goggles to fly my own plane, listlessly sailing among the clouds. Several years later, I was to get acquainted with the single-winged enclosed Piper Cub and Taylorcraft, but my heart was still with the oldies and their noisy engines.

During mid-summer, Dad, Junior and I set out on a two-day fishing trip into the virgin wilderness of Cold River Flow. We had packed more than enough food for two days, simple fishing tackle and bait, plus some basic utensils and a hatchet. Then, as a final precaution, tossed in a first-aid kit and a couple of extra blankets.

If I remember correctly, we left the car near Tahawus, in the heart of the Adirondacks, and took a trail the five miles or so to Moose Pond. From there, it was about another five miles to Cold River, which was the domain of Noah Rondeau, the renowned Hermit of Cold River Flow. Except for brief visits to civilization for basic supplies, he lived in the far wilderness year around. In years to come, a replica of his rustic cabin would be displayed at the Adirondack Museum in Blue Mountain Lake, New York.

The summer had been unseasonably hot and dry, making the stream a little more than a trickle of water. Some of the rocky pockets contained water warm enough to bathe in. The trout had evidently moved either downstream or out to the connecting ponds into deeper, and consequently cooler, water. With this disappointing situation, we decided to return to

Moose Pond, spend the night there, and try fishing the pond in the morning when it wouldn't be as warm. There was also a state lean-to near the water, which would provide shelter.

By the time we hiked back to the pond, we were pretty well tuckered out, and hungry to boot! After stowing our gear in the lean-to, Junior began gathering up some pieces of wood for a fire in the outdoor stone fireplace. As he was squatting down to split some kindling, the hatchet suddenly glanced off one of the larger sticks, burying the corner of the blade into his leg, just above the knee cap.

Here we were, five miles from the car, and who knows how far from a doctor! We started with compresses until the bleeding subsided, then squeezed the slit together, holding it closed with adhesive tape. We knew that it wouldn't be feasible to try getting out at night; we would need to stay until morning. Dad coated the wound with iodine from the first aid kit, then put a fresh piece of tape with gauze underneath directly over the gash. We wound an entire roll of gauze tightly around Junior's leg, and tied a bandana handkerchief over that. It was then we remarked how fortunate we were to have that first-aid kit!

We made Junior as comfortable as possible in the log structure, and then proceeded to get a fire going. Hazel and Grandmother had given us more than enough sandwiches, some fruit, and chocolate bars. We had brought along a fry pan, salt and pepper, butter, and a small kettle to heat water. The fry pan and butter were to be used for cooking the trout we were supposed to take from "warm" Cold River.

Nobody slept much that night. Junior was having nightmares, tossing and turning in his sleep, and an uninvited owl offered some unwelcome hoots. Toward morning, a distant black bear bellowed a warning for the benefit of his ego, to let the wilds know who was boss! We had no fear of the wild animals, for humans are their innate nemesis. A porcupine is one that is not to be provoked, however, especially if it has waddled into one's sleeping area and decides to nibble on some of the merchandise. It can usually be shooed out safely, as long as it is not irritated. When a safe distance away, give it some well-aimed missiles of sticks or stones to let it know that it is not welcome. It may not be back right away, but it will be back, you can be sure!

We built up the fire and heated water for tea, then toasted some of the peanut butter sandwiches for breakfast. Junior felt better, in general, but his leg hurt when he bent his knee. The wound had clotted well, but it was imperative that he keep his leg stiff while walking. Dad and I shouldered the equipment and supplies for the five-mile hike to the car, leaving Junior free to favor his game leg, using a forked sapling as a crutch.

Every half-mile or so, we would stop to rest and make sure that my brother's walking was not overly irritating the sore leg. After nearly four hours of a tedious gait, we were delighted when the car loomed ahead. With sighs of relief, we loaded the baggage into the vehicle, leaving room for Junior to sit with his leg resting across the seat.

As soon as we arrived home, the bandages were removed and fresh dressings applied to the apparently uninfected wound. Grandmother and Hazel were both shocked, but thankful that we had that first-aid kit along! Our doctor mentioned that the gash should have had stitches, but as long as it appeared to be healing well he said, "Let it be." We all learned a very important lesson from that adventure: No matter how inconsequential an outing may seem, always have a first-aid kit within reach, as a part of the camping equipment, and in the vehicle!

This hot, dry weather was ideal for the farmers' haying season, and with the old adage, "You have to make hay while the sun shines," it was crucial to get it cut, air dried and into the barn as quickly as possible. A rainstorm could delay the operation indefinitely, so I volunteered to help my friend, Harold, and his Uncle Ed, get in the hay already cut and drying in their field.

In those days, hay was loaded onto the large hay wagon by pitchfork, each fork-full carefully overlapping the previous one. This locked the hay shocks in place for the trip to the barn. If one fork-full was not in its proper place, the top half of the load could slip off. That happened on our first load (and was probably my fault). Harold's uncle halted the horses, slid down off the remaining load, threw his straw hat onto the ground and headed for the barn on foot.

By the time Harold and I had reloaded the wagon, his uncle returned, and as if nothing had happened, climbed back to the top of the load. His only remark was "Gid-dap" to the horses with a snap of the reins.

As we walked toward the barn, Harold mentioned that he didn't have conclusive evidence, but surmised that Uncle Ed might have a jug of home brew stashed somewhere close by; consequently, his altered disposition! The work went well from

then on, and Ed even seemed quite congenial. I acquired a painful sunburn that first day by leaving my shirt off too long. Being of fair complexion, I should have been more cautious, but Harold just got nicely tanned. I worked with my shirt on, and wearing a wide-brimmed straw hat for the remaining hay days, but was sore and peeling for a week later. Just another example of learning by doing.

The remaining days of summer were taken up by a mixture of work and recreational activities. Junior and I alternated the duties of the ice cream parlor, the lawn work and family needs. Swimming, baseball games, fishing, and mixed night outings just about covered the fun part. Of course, sleeping late was happiness in itself!

On some evenings in late summer we enjoyed corn roasts. A group of a dozen or more fellows and girls would collect fresh, unhusked corn, potato salad, cole slaw, butter, salt and pepper, and Coca Cola or some other soft drink. We would get together at some out-of-the-way location, such as the swimming hole beach, county campground or any other convenient place to have an open fire. The corn would be roasted in its husk, then peeled to expose the steaming kernels.

After stuffing ourselves with the hot buttered corn, salad and slaw, we would sing songs and dance barefoot in the sand. When things began to die down, we would sit around the fire and talk about subjects relating to everyday life—topics that our parents had yet to credit us with knowing. We enjoyed each other's company and respected each other, which made our youthful bonds evolve into lasting friendships for years to come.

I really looked forward to my final year of high school with anticipation and a deep feeling of accomplishment in the eleven years that had brought me that far. I was determined to do my very best this term, with the heavy load of studies ahead of me. I was also to be the pitcher on our high school varsity baseball team.

Junior was beginning his junior year, but had been struggling with a number of subjects carried over. He was determined to graduate, even if it took an extra semester to do it!

Bobbie was excited about his first year in elementary school. He felt that if Junior and I could do it, so could he! I had always hoped that we were setting a good example for him during his first six years. He had always shown interest in our activities.

Loren, the school bus driver, asked me to drive his car to the high school in the morning, and back home after school in the afternoon, on the days when he wasn't on duty. By doing this, he'd have use of the auto during the day while at home. The bus had to be left at school during school hours, but at his home at night.

It was understood that I would carry no riders, which was all right with me; Loren also understood that I might be a little late on afternoons having a basketball game or practice. I would always let him know ahead of time, as some of the games would finish very late.

I was delighted to drive that new DeSoto Airflow sedan, that appeared at first glance to be a bathtub upside down. It handled like a dream, with comfort galore. I needed to ride the bus only about one week out of the month, and was not only envied by my classmates, but had also gained the trust of my elders.

Junior and I looked forward to yet another hunting season, which would soon be upon us. It would be my brother's first license to hunt with a rifle—the .25/20 which I had replaced with a .30 caliber autoloader. Dad had bought the latter from a fellow who said there was something wrong with it that he couldn't fix. Dad's rifle was exactly the same, except that his was a .32 caliber, and he was familiar with every part of it. He gave the fellow five dollars for the gun, and took it apart to find the trouble. After he had reassembled it, it was as good as new. He had nothing to say about the impairment, nor did any one of us ask. It has never failed me in all the years since.

There was one mix-up with our rifles, that I distinctly remember. Dad and I each had identical looped shell belts containing shells that appeared the same, except that mine were .30 caliber and his .32. I have no idea how the belts got switched, but after we entered the woods, I found that my shells wouldn't slide into the rifle chamber. I examined the cartridge and saw .32 REM stamped on the rim. I knew that my .30's would slide loosely into his rifle, and if fired, could explode in the breach. That would be a disaster!

I took off running in the direction Dad and Junior had taken, yelling at the top of my lungs. After I found them, I asked Dad to look at his shells. He appeared as if he thought I had gone berserk, but after a close scrutiny, he unloaded his rifle and we switched belts. My yelling probably scared every living creature from the area, but perhaps prevented a serious mishap. From then on, we checked our ammo very carefully!

As in previous seasons, our woodland excursions were limited to the weekends or holidays. High winds or rain were deterrents in deer hunting season, while snow and cold, though uncomfortable, were readily tolerated. We were counting on Thanksgiving vacation to do the bulk of our deer hunting, with hopes that the weather would cooperate.

Since the big-game season opened on October 25th, Dad had been on several successful hunts with a few of his cohorts. Although he didn't admit shooting anything, there was often venison to be divided up. Someone in the group seemed to get lucky every few days!

On weekends, Junior and I would join the group, helping out with the deer drives. We would see deer quite often, but usually the part that goes over the fence last, without showing antlers. We would never shoot at a deer unless we knew that it was a deer—and legal. That was a very important part of our training.

More deer were shot at than put down. Deer don't give hunters a chance for a shot—as if deer should stand pat and take their chances! It rarely happens, but at times an alert hunter will get a couple of seconds to get a shot off before his prey leaps for cover.

# Chapter 20

The December that I turned eighteen was a milestone in my life. Though my brother and I had tasted beer and tobacco, we were not impressed by either. Now that I was legally "of age," I was not influenced by the temptation of being able to step over the line. If it were to become of interest at some later time, I would deal with it then.

The tourist business was comparably light through the fall and winter, but Dad's taxidermy work was expanding. Deer hides were tanned and made into gloves, jackets and moccasins, which Dad and Hazel sold for generous profits. Bear skin rugs, small mounted birds and animals also were becoming popular items, along with specialized mounted deer heads. Most of the leather items were manufactured during the winter and then marketed in summer when tourists were abundant.

The new Whiteface Mountain Memorial Highway, a few miles away, seemed to be enticing travelers to the rooming houses, stores, and restaurants in the area. With this bonanza, Dad and Hazel leased a small restaurant near the foot of the mountain in the early spring. They remodeled it and made it into a small diner, with living quarters, which they planned on opening for business in June. Dad, Hazel and Bobbie would be living there during the busy summer season.

That left Junior and me and Grandmother to keep the old homestead in operation. By the time that the summer season arrived, a young woman Dad had hired, and her man-friend, moved in to help out. Rosie was an able, neat worker, but Mac was a slob! It was not difficult for us to predict the length of that relationship! Rosie gave Mac his walking papers to save her job, and he begrudgingly left, not to return for the rest of the summer. Grandmother and Rosie were quite compatible, especially after Rosie understood who was boss! She was very considerate and helpful to Grandmother, who appreciated every minute of it.

After graduation from high school in late June, I took a job as a custodian of the local elementary school. It was a part-time position, which entailed taking over the duties of the retiring custodian.

Until September, the bulk of the work was mowing the lawns around the school building and the adjoining baseball field. This had to be done about once a week with an old gasoline-powered reel-type mower with a 24-inch cut. According to my figures, I followed that machine over five miles each mowing! Often times the drive chain would fly off, and extra time was required to replace the greasy reject.

One time when Junior was helping out with the mowing, and the old mower chain was repeatedly falling off, he picked it up and, with expletives not fit to print, flung it as far as he could into an adjacent hay field! After a lengthy search, we found it and subsequently turned the problem over to the District Superintendent. The machine was gone for a couple days, during which time I had visions of a brand new mower. But that was not to be—the same old relic came back with a new, snug-fitting drive chain.

With the custodian work, tending the soda fountain and other chores around home, Junior and I had little time to have fun. As Rosie became more acclimated to the work at the restaurant, she relieved us of the soda fountain tasks, much to our gratification. When the weather cooperated, we had lawn work to do—mine at the school, and Junior's at the homes of, now his, regular customers.

Inclement weather didn't interfere with our fishing unless a bad thunderstorm was brewing. However, after a hard rainstorm we found the trout more receptive to our bait, and usually brought in a couple of the larger ones. Grandmother had a special touch for cooking them, which made the flesh fall conveniently off the bones. How I hated to find fish bones in my fillets! I guess that's why I always enjoyed eating sardines.

As the summer progressed, I noticed that Rosie was becoming most attentive and interested in my outside activities and would often get close to me when nobody else was near. It didn't concern me too much, as my girl friends in high school did that too, but it did seem a bit unusual for an older gal! Then early one evening, as I was leaving to join our friends for a corn roast, Rosie leaned over the soda fountain, tenderly kissed me on the lips and whispered that she hoped I would have a nice time!

How can a fellow possibly enjoy an outing with his friends, while visions of impropriety are floating through his mind? Though I might have appeared insensitive to party activities, nobody seemed to notice. When I returned home, Rosie had gone to bed and, in a way, I was thankful. I didn't have to face her that night, but I knew that sooner or later I must!

In the days that followed, nothing much was implied that would visibly stimulate a relationship, but feelings can be transmitted through sensory channels, I'm sure! A few evenings later, Rosie mentioned to Grandmother that she would like to go for a walk, but would rather not go alone. Out of the goodness in her heart, Grandmother volunteered my services. Of course Rosie had this planned all along!

After we were out of sight down the darkened street, she took my hand in hers, and we slowly walked to the school house where we sat on the front steps. We talked about our respective lives in general—mine quite adventurous—her's more complex and confused. Through the understanding of each other's expectations, viewpoints and desires, a mutual bond was formed, relaxing my attitude toward her. We both knew now, that a closer relationship between us was apparent.

In the few weeks of summer during our evening walks, Rosie taught me aspects of life that would have ordinarily appeared later in life. I accepted, and returned her tokens of endearment, with no regrets then or ever. When she had to leave in the early fall, it felt as if we were the hypothetical ships that pass in the night, for we both knew it was the way it had to be.

When Bobbie started his second year in the local elementary school, Dad and Hazel stayed at the house nights and traveled to "The Little Restaurant" in Wilmington, mornings. A helper opened the diner to serve breakfast before they would arrive. It was expected that the diner would stay open until mid-October, in order to reap some business from the tour-bus loads of autumn leaf-watchers.

Junior had a full schedule in his senior year and, with or without help, it appeared that he would need an extra semester to complete his degree. His determination was still present, in spite of the adversities. We were all proud of him.

My work as school custodian entailed cleaning the two classrooms, the bathrooms and halls each evening, raising and lowering the flag each day, and keeping the automatically-fed coal furnace operating efficiently. When winter set in, there would be driveways to clear of snow, and walks to shovel, in addition to the regular duties. This work, as with the taxidermy art, was not appealing as my life's work. My future was yet to be determined, based upon my wishes and capabilities.

Most of our deer hunting that fall was squeezed between Dad's backed-up shop work, my custodial job, and Junior's school attendance. On a few good days, Dad and I might still-hunt separate areas to cover more territory in a short time, or locate likely spots to just sit and watch.

On one of those watches, where I had seen deer tracks crossing an old, narrow dirt road, I picked a spot down-wind from the deer trail and made myself comfortable. That is, as comfortable as one can be while sitting on a cold, rough piece of granite! It was beginning to get dusky there among the spruces, making it necessary for me to fold down the rear peep-sight on my .30 Remington, and tip up the middle open sight to improve visibility. As I made the change, I caught a glimpse of something walking across the road with its nose down, apparently sniffing a former deer trail.

I could barely see the deer in my sights, but I fired. The buck humped as if something had hit him in the belly, and jumped into the brushy growth. I knew the bullet had hit him, but where, and how badly? It is always best, in a case such as this, to sit and wait for the animal to lie down, with the hope that, given time, it would succumb to the damaging wound.

Waiting for something like this makes the time drag, but it was getting darker by the minute. I walked over to the point where the deer disappeared and carefully entered the woods, scrutinizing the area ahead. With the darkness and thickets of small trees, I felt it unlikely that I would find the buck, even if at my feet! Then, no more than a dozen feet away, there was an explosion of leaves and brush as the animal jumped up and bounded off. I had no chance for a shot.

After marking the road with the toe of my boot, I walked to the car and drove home. I sadly recounted the experience to the family, with Dad stating that we would return there early the next morning and track from there. It could be possible that the buck laid down further on, and that we would find him there, dead.

When we returned to the trail, we found that the deer was definitely hit, for there was some blood where I had seen him the evening before. We followed his tracks for over a half-mile, but there was no sign of a slowed gait. We left the trail with hopes that the deer would survive. There are always if's about situations that can change the complete picture, and there were at least a couple of them here!

# Chapter 21

I remember years ago when our next door neighbor, Don, and I were planning a trip to Tahiti as soon as we finished high school. We would be buying a motorcycle, packing the minimum in personal items, and whizzing out to San Francisco. There we would sell the bike to buy passage on the next ship that would drop us off at that paradise in the tropical South Pacific! Once in Tahiti, we would need only a small thatched hut, just above the high tide mark, and be served by the suntanned, skimpily adorned native beauties.

By the time I graduated from high school, Don had been through two post-graduate years, taking every subject except Home Economics, which he left to the girls. He then became interested in a Federal Government job. Even now, I dream of that fantastic trip with sighs of remorse, then reluctantly check it off as a figment of our expansive imaginations. But by then, I was almost twenty, and maybe I could get Don to change his mind!

Those warm thoughts provided little consolation when I looked outside to see snow, icicles hanging from eaves, and people with scarves over their mouths to avoid breathing that cold Arctic wind!

The previous fall Dad had purchased a twenty-five-acre farm at a tax sale, then obtained a secure title from the registered owner. The farmhouse had not been occupied for quite some time and was beyond repair, but the acreage appeared valuable. A small brook gurgled happily by the house from the hills to the west and joined a larger stream farther east. The water was clear and cold, being fed by springs on the hillside far above.

While deer hunting in that area, I noticed several sugar maples of various sizes that appeared to have been tapped at some time in the past. I began to think about producing maple syrup. In a few weeks, hopefully, the sap would be running, and I wanted to be a part of harvesting this product of nature. The previous spring, maple syrup producers were getting up to three dollars a gallon for that delicious, sweet liquid. An energetic fellow, such as I, could make a fortune from those maples on the farm!

Of course we all know that maple syrup doesn't come directly from maple trees, any more than cottage cheese comes directly from cows! In both cases, there is a process involved, which leads to hard work. The whole idea is to be crafty enough to catch the sap flowing up from the tree roots before it reaches the limbs. We also know that most of the maple sap gets up there anyway, otherwise there would be no leaves later!

Equipment needed to be assembled: We needed spouts and buckets, large storage containers for the gathered sap, a large rectangular pan for boiling it, and a fireplace upon which to set the pan. I'd need fuel to burn under the sap-filled pan to evaporate the water and cause the sap to thicken into syrup. Sounds like fun, right? Only time would tell!

I didn't want to get into this on too large a scale and flood the market with that sweet stuff! That would bring the prices down. So I bought a couple dozen sap buckets (with covers, in case of rain) and the same amount of spouts, from a former syrup producer who had gone out of business.

Our old Model-A Ford pickup truck furnished my transportation to and from the "sugar bush." I'd bring my daily collection home, where the pan would be set up, making it a mite easier to boil at night if necessary.

I made the boiling pan from a three by eight-foot piece of sheet iron, bending the edges up about seven inches, crimping them for strength, then took it to the local garage for soldering the overlaps. Two layers of old concrete blocks furnished a wall to receive the pan, which allowed about fifteen inches underneath for the fire. Oh, yes, the fire. From the ice house sawmill, I bought a truckload of slabs cut from tree logs. They provided a hot bed of coals and kept the sap boiling.

The family members had little to say about my undertaking, but there was some head-shaking and muttering. I had used up practically all of my meager savings, but couldn't help thinking of those enormous profits to come!

About a week later, the weather began to change, favoring the start of the sugaring season. Air temperatures were warming during the sunny days, with freezing thermometer readings at night—ideal conditions for the sap to run. In view of this, I eagerly plodded through knee-deep snow to my towering maples. Those majestic monarchs were selected for tapping by their size and abundance of limbs in the crowns. That would allow at least two buckets to hang on each tree.

As the trees were some distance apart, it required a stomped-down trail from tree to tree, and to the truck several yards down the hill. Oh well, I didn't expect it to be easy, so a little extra work shouldn't put a crimp in the ultimate result.

With my bit brace and auger, sap spouts and buckets, I toured my prepacked trail in a circular pattern, boring holes and pounding in the sap spouts. Each tapping was wet with sap, proving that conditions were at their best. It was getting late and I needed to return to my custodial work, so there were only a half-dozen buckets catching drips as I left.

The following day, I managed to install the remaining hardware, setting three taps on some of the extra large trees. Buckets hung late the day before were less than half full, making only one trip with the gathering pails necessary. It would be another day or two before the system was producing in volume, but I'd be ready! The boiling pan was set up in the garden area, with a large canvas tent fly available to throw over a framework, in the event of rain.

It took about three days of gathering to fill the two thirty-gallon metal barrels, one of which would be transferred to the pan. Fortunately, this important procedure would be ready when Junior volunteered his services to tend the fire and keep a sharp eye on the boiling process. Dad began to take interest also, much to my gratification and joy! I was glad to have him aboard the bonanza wagon! I was beginning to speculate that all of this hard work was not in vain after all. Or was it?

While the boiling was taking place, I was gathering more and more of that maple liquid each day. The tent fly proved its worth on a couple of rainy days, but gathering was getting to be a wet, sloppy mess. The runs started slowing down as the weather warmed, and it was evident that it was necessary to "pull the plug." We had nearly a hundred gallons to boil yet and I had to buy another load of slab-wood to keep the fire going. However, that would be the final expense for the project.

When every drop had been boiled and the buckets, spouts and containers washed and put away, we had made seven gallons of syrup. I had planned on selling the fruits of my labors for four dollars a gallon, but now I found that, with my costs for equipment, firewood, gas for the truck—not counting my time—the syrup cost me eleven dollars per gallon!

I crossed off one more occupation on my list of possible vocations.

# Chapter 22

In early summer, Dad had an offer from an Italian family to purchase our restaurant and tourist home. However, the prospective owners requested permission to move in and operate the business on a trial basis, pending funding. They would pay a reasonable amount in monthly installments until the final contract was negotiated.

Dad agreed and we moved our personal items, furniture, equipment, and supplies to a house about a half-mile away. Grandmother, Junior and I lived there during the summer, while Dad, Hazel and Bobbie occupied "The Little Restaurant" in Wilmington and returned to join us in the fall.

Junior and I were occupied with our summer work, me with the school upkeep and my brother with his lawn work and odd jobs around town. Of course we allowed time for swimming, fishing, or just loafing around. I had use of the Ford pick-up, which I shared with Junior when absolutely necessary.

Dad depended on us to look after Grandmother, who was now past her mid-eighties, though she wouldn't admit it. There was little evidence by her actions that she was not as spry as always. We made it a rule for at least one of us to be nearby at all times, or away for only short periods. We made no fuss about it, knowing full well that she had been a most important part of our lives through our motherless years.

By the time fall arrived, the property buyer reneged on the purchase agreement for our sorely missed homestead. Because the business was located next to a church, the prospective owner wasn't granted a license to sell liquor. This, apparently, was the chief deterrent to his changing his mind. They moved out, and we moved back in! Our neighbors were as pleased as we were with the outcome, and offered their assistance in getting us settled once more.

It seemed that we had just been away for the summer and were returning to our home. Dad and Hazel went back on their schedule of days in Wilmington and nights at home until mid-October, when the diner was closed for the winter. Dad then went back to the shop and caught up on the taxidermy work.

At that period in my life, I was becoming more aware of

the challenges and possibilities of the future. Being a school custodian aroused little, if any, stimulation for me. I began thinking about finding more satisfying employment for myself, and was alert for opportunities.

With my routine tasks at the school taking up my early morning and late afternoon hours, my deer hunting was limited to mid-day or weekends. Deer, as with most animals, bed down in mid-day and do their foraging at alternate intervals. Most hunters consider this period less productive and use that time to take a break and rest up. A still-hunter, who moves along stealthily at a slow gait, can often find this dull time quite advantageous.

Unless I was a participant in a hunting party, I preferred using my own still-hunting abilities when stalking those four-legged, cud-chewing animals. By slowly and carefully walking, stopping, looking, and proceeding with the wind, the chances of spotting any deer were excellent. While using that system of stalking, it was surprising to notice other interesting parts of the natural environment. A peculiar rock formation would catch my eye, or an animal of another species would show itself, unaware of human presence. The wonders of nature are endless to those who respect and enjoy them!

There was a relatively small mountain in our area that was an ideal bedding area for deer, having steep, practically inaccessible ledges on adjacent sides. When alerted by a hunter approaching from the less difficult side, the deer would bound off in divergent directions, with the ledges being the major escape route. After having witnessed this strategy before, I decided that an unorthodox method of stalking was in order. It could be difficult, and rather inane, but worth a try. One never knows the outcome without some effort extended!

Weatherwise it was an unusual morning for mid-November. There was a trace of snow, covered by a coat of ice from freezing rain. I had made my plans to scale that mountain that day, but then it appeared doubtful. After the morning school tasks were completed, however, the conditions seemed a little more favorable and I decided to go for it.

The wheel-track dirt road was icy, but the old Ford, with some persuasion, dutifully transported me to a point some distance from the base of the mountain. Conditions at the higher elevation were not pleasant either. The tree limbs had a heavy coating of ice. With weather like this, there had to be a white-tail hiding up there. With my sandwich and apple tucked into the back of my jacket, I put shells into the magazine of my rifle and carefully began climbing toward the rocky face of the mountain. My preplanned course of action was based on a route to the top, contrary to the conventional access, which had proved accommodating for the deer. I was going to invade their backyard by ascending the ledges that had allowed them to slip away so easily.

Scaling those rocky outcrops with their narrow shelves and jagged surfaces would have been a tedious undertaking even with dry footing, but now it was icy and seemingly impassable. However, with slow and deliberate steps from one foothold to the next, I determined that I was gaining elevation quite well. More than once I thought of turning back, but descending would be more treacherous than continuing upward. When I noticed that the slope was becoming less impregnable, I quietly injected one of the cartridges into the rifle chamber. Should the need arise for a quick shot, I would only need to press the safety to off.

As I peered over the last flat rock at the summit, my eyes caught a movement in some dense scotch pines about thirty yards away. In one small spot about a foot wide, at irregular intervals, I could see the side of a face—an eye, ear and part of an antler. In a fleeting second or two it would be visible, then disappear! One fact that I did understand was that the "thing" was a whitetail deer—and a buck to boot! I was also sure that he was not aware of my presence. The problem was, how would I get a shot at him?

The alternatives at hand were few: I could wait him out until he was ready to get up on his feet, which could be an hour or more, or I might slowly slink at an angle away from him, with a chance for a shot as he leaped out of his bed. My best chance, I concluded, was to shoot at what I saw—when I saw it! If I missed, perhaps the sound would startle him, but not drive him away too far.

It was a small target to aim at, but I rested the rifle on the large rock hiding me and waited for his head to show. When it again came into view, I adjusted my aim to the base of his ear, then it disappeared again. At least now I had the sights on that spot for his next move. In a few seconds his head came into view and I squeezed the trigger. Apparently his head was at a different angle that time, and I missed. He bounded off, more startled than fearful, out of sight into the thick evergreens.

While hunting with Dad, my brother and I had learned

many helpful hints on deer hunting, one of which was, in an event such as this, to give the deer time to settle down. Whenever he halted his stride, one could be certain that he would be watching and waiting to find out what disturbed him.

After what seemed like an hour (maybe fifteen minutes) I slowly and very carefully moved, looking left, right and forward. In front of me, and to my left, were more dwarfed pines. Off to my right, the woods opened up to a stand of hardwoods. I had the notion that he had gone through the open timber to a thicket farther down. His tracks appeared to lead in that direction. As I was studying the hardwood area, I heard a snort a few yards ahead, and got a glimpse of the buck leaping down the hill in the opposite direction. Then I knew for sure, after seeing me, he wasn't stopping again until he was far, far away! I had no chance for a shot.

I had outwitted the buck by precariously climbing the ledges to his backdoor, but he outsmarted me in the end. Crestfallen with the results, but having confidence in the methods employed, my spirits were not entirely at ground level. I decided to eat my lunch before still-hunting my way back down the more gentle slope of the mountain.

In the woods, I usually toasted my sandwich over a small fire, but with the trees and underbrush covered with ice, it was difficult to find dry twigs or birch bark for kindling. However, by crawling under some thick spruces and breaking off dry, dead limbs, I collected enough tinder for a fair-sized fire, and whittled a forked stick for toasting my sandwich.

With that cozy, snapping, crackling respite, I felt a certain amount of solace—until I reached for my lunch in the back of my jacket. It was not there! I must have lost it while climbing the ledges. That was the theoretical straw that broke the camel's back! I kicked the hard-earned fire half-way down the icy slope as I trudged wearily and dejectedly to my dependable old truck parked below. On the way home, I could almost hear Dad's expression, "Chalk it up to experience!"

# Chapter 23

With several months of inclement weather ahead, I thought about obtaining some additional education in a field that would be interesting and productive. While tossing the idea around in my head, I remembered the praise Uncle Leslie bestowed upon me regarding my artistic ability, several years back. Art would be an exciting, enjoyable, as well as an interesting field. Why not give it a try?

Before the notion cooled off, I signed up with the Federal Schools, Inc., of Minneapolis, for a correspondence course in Illustrating and Cartooning. For the moment at least, I was the master of my destiny! The twelve divisions covered just about every phase of art, from show-card work and drawing cartoons, to real life subjects in various mediums. Dad wasn't a bit enthused with my choice of study, as he had pictured me in a suit, with an armful of lawyer's legal briefs, on my way to court! To allay his apprehension, I simply remarked that if and when I got this idea out of my system, I would consider his wishes.

While keeping up the custodial work at the Elementary School and my progress in the art course, I managed to get some showcard advertising work at a few businesses in surrounding towns. There wasn't much compensation involved in it, but I thought it might develop into a more lucrative practice later on. With this roseate outlook, how could one not enjoy the work?

Throughout the winter, I was getting good grades on the work that was submitted for criticism. I was sure that I could never be another Norman Rockwell, Walter Wilwerding, or Fontaine Fox, and that my work would be no more than satisfactory, but I was as smug as a squirrel in a tree full of nuts! As I mentioned earlier, had I depended upon this as my life's work, I would have starved to death! There was no chance of becoming rich, monetarily, only the wealth of self-satisfaction was my reward.

Art studies formed another stepping stone and provided a branch of learning that produced an appreciation for entering a world that was seemingly above and beyond the ordinary. It added a flash of insight that I had never experienced before, and gave me a feeling of peace within.

I reached my twentieth birthday in early December, while Junior would be nineteen the following March. He still struggled with his study load, but was able to finish high school in June with credits to spare. There had been little mention of what he intended thereafter, but with trouble brewing in Europe, who knew what would happen.

After suffering last spring's financial embarrassment with my maple syrup fiasco, I scuttled all thoughts of that undertaking again in the spring. Of course, I had the equipment, and we still possessed some of the most expensive maple syrup in the country, rating it with the exclusive, and distinguished European wines! We used it conservatively and on special occasions.

Along with our extra studies and activities, my brother Junior and I always managed to find time for helping Grandmother. Even at her age, she still took delight in her garden. We did most of the work by then, but she still prided herself in raising the most productive plants in town!

Junior and I had purchased our hunting and fishing licenses that fall, and were all set for our annual bout with the cold, roiled water of the AuSable. We intended to give Bobbie a taste of the rigors that go with early spring fishing during the first weekend of the season. I personally preferred fly fishing later on, but still got the urge to fight the elements and hook some big brown trout as well. We had learned through experience that being at the river that first day of fishing season was not only uncomfortable, but unproductive as well.

Bobbie and Junior had collected an ample supply of angleworms from Grandmother's garden, and were getting fishing tackle organized for the coming weekend. There was always a need for snelled hooks and sinkers. In all probability, there were dozens of them wrapped around rocks and snags along the river bottom from previous seasons! The general store usually kept a good supply of the simple items on hand that were required for bait angling, including metal rods, reels, and bamboo poles.

The river water was ice cold, with irregular chunks of ice cast haphazardly along the banks—having been deposited by the angry, swollen stream. This condition was expected and tolerated annually, as mentioned before.

Junior showed Bobbie how to bait his hook, and gave him

some instructions on casting, letting the lure set awhile, then retrieving to check bait and cast to an alternate location. It brought back memories of several years ago when Junior and I were going through this oft-times painful process! My hands still ached from the ice-water, and one wonders if it was really worth the discomfort. But we felt that it *was* worth it, and we always went back for more!

I was using my fly rod and a small brass spinner with a light colored streamer fly behind as a lure representing a minnow. It had worked well in reasonably clear water, but I wanted to give it a try in this murky stream. Casting down and across the current, and retrieving in jerks seemed to be the on-going method with the streamer. Junior and Bobbie were getting some light bumps, but the trout seemed listless and indifferent, probably due to the low water temperature.

We finally decided that it was useless to continue under these rough and adverse conditions, but would go back later, when the water cleared. As the two reeled in, I made one final cast far out and across the fast current. I worked the lure back in, putting as much action as possible into the tempting bait. Suddenly, there was a terrific yank, and my vibrating rod was bent with the struggle of a large fish. It took several minutes to tire and force the thrashing, finned beauty into our net. The beautiful cold-water brown trout was over sixteen inches long, and weighed just over two pounds. That episode proved that it's the cast that catches the fish that makes your day!

Experiences such as this cause ordinary humans to react by wearing outlandish outfits, adorned with a multitude of barbed foreign objects, and to lose sense of time. Medical research would be at a loss in seeking a cure for this malady, which in itself provides temporary relief from all sorts of adverse conditions. Whether one is nine or ninety, male or female, the bug is there! Once one is bitten, there is no antidote! From small mountain brooks, to ponds, lakes and the ocean, angling takes on many forms and styles, each producing the same overpowering sensitivity of freedom and self-content to all.

During May and June, Dad hired a local Wilmington couple to manage the diner, while he and Hazel tended to the influx of customers at our tourist home. There were several professional fishermen, most with wives, who took advantage of the favorable weather and water conditions for testing their equipment in the AuSable. The results were usually satisfactory for proving the effectiveness of the rods, reels, line, leaders, and lures of the companies they represented. It was imperative that we made them feel comfortable in our pleasant surroundings, for the tourist home was often mentioned in some of their literary accounts.

Throughout the summer, Dad kept the helpers at the diner and flitted back and forth between the two business establishments daily. One evening, Dad mentioned that he had met someone who was vacationing at the Wilmington Inn, across the street from the diner, whom he wanted me to meet.

On the way over to the diner the next morning, he announced that the mysterious stranger was the Personnel Manager of the General Electric Company in Schenectady. He then disclosed that he and the stranger had had a conversation regarding a certain young man who was seeking gainful employment.

When the gentleman appeared for his mid-morning coffee, I tried not to be nervous or to show anxiety. After Dad introduced us, the gent invited me to sit at his table, where we began discussing fishing, hunting and the Adirondacks. I soon overcame my uneasiness and began asking about his family, the city, and commonplace subjects. It was as if I were conversing with a well-known acquaintance.

After a time, the topic of employment came up along with my experience and the type of work I was interested in. He asked if I were looking for the money or longevity in the company. "Both," I answered without delay.

With a grin, he winked at Dad and left with the statement, "Come down and see me when you're twenty-one."

My whole body tingled with excitement, mixed with some self-restraint, remembering my commitments at home and my school obligations.

For the remaining days of summer and early fall, Junior, Bobbie and I did some fishing—they with the usual baits and I with my favorite evening fly casting. Other than our regular seasonal jobs, we did some berry picking for Grandmother's preserves and helped with the gardening. In addition to the harvesting of vegetables, we gathered surplus apples from a local orchard, which were canned, and the peelings made into a delicious jelly. Obtaining venison for the winter was assigned to the—now three—hunters of the family. This was the one chore that we always looked forward to. Junior was through school and would no longer be restricted to weekend hunting.

The mountains were aflame with nature's unfailing annual display of reds, yellows, and blended shades not to be found on the artist's palette! In a few days, rain and wind would destroy this result of months of effort by the hardwoods.

During the first week of November, Dad, Junior and I packed a few essentials and proceeded to the Maynard camp, where five years before, we were unarmed side-kicks. Now, it was the real thing, and being there during the week, rather than the weekend, would provide a better than usual opportunity to bag a deer. Jim and Mary had the camp set up before the big-game season opened, but hadn't looked around much to estimate the whitetail population in the area.

We were planning on staying two or three days, with Paul, one of Dad's hunting companions, driving up to hunt for a day or so. He had a garage business to manage, making his mid-week outings limited.

That first evening watch didn't produce any venison, although there were several animals roaming around—all does and fawns from what we were able to determine. The bucks were hanging back until after dark.

We had brought some prepared food dishes from home, as well as some baked items, but Mary was ahead of us! It was chicken and dumplings, with fruit salad and vegetables. We were all well stuffed, and just wanted to relax, but a hint from Dad was enough to put Junior and I at the dishpan!

Waking up to the smell of coffee and frying bacon before daylight is an experience we had been familiar with before, but in a tent-frame camp in the wilderness, the hunger became acute. Then, as the flap-jacks bubbled and flopped, we began to drool! The night before we wouldn't believe we could eat another bite, yet here we were all over again. Wow! What a way to live!

It was just before sunrise when the four of us walked up the wheel-track road toward the park line. Jim took a trail off to one side, where he had a favorite spot near a well-used deer runway; we continued on to the park line. There, several small deer bounded off in different directions—none with antlers. Junior took the line trail to the right, Dad and I spread out farther up the left trail. We were all to meet back at camp by noon, then rest up before going back out for the afternoon watch.

Jim had seen a small buck with some does, but didn't shoot, supposing there would be a bigger one hanging back until the "coast was clear," but it never showed. Dad and I had no luck, but Junior said he had seen the track of a large buck that had crossed the trail recently. He planned on being at that spot again in the afternoon and tomorrow morning, just in case the old fellow tried the same route again.

Paul arrived about noontime and would get in on the late afternoon watch and again tomorrow morning. Then we would, reluctantly, be heading for home.

We spread out along the park line, as before, hoping that a nice buck would decide to commit suicide in the presence of one of us, but no such luck! The problem here is that you cannot legally shoot a deer in the park without a special permit from the owners, and if you have a permit, you will be over there where the deer spend most of their time. But if one is shot on the state side, then goes over there to fall down, you have the right to retrieve it. Line walkers, employed by the park owners enforce the rules whenever possible, but are quite fair in their decisions.

We enjoyed another delicious dinner, and after exchanging some bygone experiences and getting the housekeeping chores completed, we turned in for the night. We would get out early in the morning for our final, and hopefully, successful watch, then pack up for the trip home. Except for the crackling fire in the cookstove and the gentle swishing of the breeze through the spruces, the night was calm and peaceful.

Another huge breakfast was consumed before daylight had made its appearance, which made one almost want to surrender any physical exertion and leave the pristine environment to the animals! But, of course, that was not to be, especially when this was to be our last bout with the wily whitetails for this trip.

We had all hardly got settled into our favorite spots, when two rifle shots rang out from the direction Junior had taken. Paul was closest to that location, so took a walk that way to investigate. There stood my beaming and excited brother, with a beautiful ivory-antlered buck! His persistence had paid off when the animal attempted to cross the trail one more time, and failed!

We were all as proud of Junior as he was of the eight-point trophy. Dad brought the car up the road to the trail, where we had dragged the dressed out carcass, and loaded it onto the right front fender, trying it securely in place. We had some coffee at camp, and bid farewell to our hosts. We really hated to leave, but the weekend was coming up with scores of deer hunters who would be thrashing about through the brush and overrunning the trails, driving any sensible deer to the sanctuary of the private park. That was not for us, for we enjoyed the peace and quiet that Mother Nature so eloquently provided.

Being in a hurry to get home, Paul started out ahead of us and was soon out of sight. I was driving our car with Dad and his rifle in the passenger side and Junior in the back seat with the luggage. Just before reaching a large pond a few miles north of Paul Smiths, a whitetail buck came out of the woods on the right, less than fifty yards away. He stopped abruptly, then turned and bounded back into the woods from whence he came.

On Dad's instructions, I put the car out on the edge of the highway and moved ahead slowly, several feet closer to the deer's exit, and then stopped. Dad got out, and leaving the door open, walked carefully along the grassy shoulder, peering intently into the dense growth. Suddenly, he squatted down, took aim and fired. He then turned to us and yelled, "We got that one too!" The deer had been hidden, with the exception of his head and neck peeking around a tree. That's all Dad needed, for he was a noted marksman, having been praised many times for his feats.

We got the deer dressed out and loaded on the left fender, tying it securely, and continued on toward home. The whole episode hadn't taken much more than a half-hour from start to finish, but what a finish! We joked about not getting another before arriving home, because we had no space to carry it, and we had used up all of our rope!

As we passed the telephone office, where Hazel worked part time, she was talking with Paul, who was informing her that we were bringing a buck home. "That's odd, Paul," she remarked, "they just drove by with two!" It didn't take Paul long to show up at the house—he just couldn't believe it! He had to see it with his own eyes.

My deer tag went on this whitetail, making my hunting finished for the season, along with Junior's. This left Dad with an unfilled license to be used for the balance of the season, should the need arise. As far as I was concerned, there were other details regarding my future to consider now.

# Chapter 24

A couple days after my twenty-first birthday, Dad, Junior, a friend of his and I drove to Schenectady for my appointment with the Personnel Director of General Electric. After a short wait in his office, filling out forms, I met with him and he seemed happy to see me again. He asked about my family, the weather up north—commonplace things. Regarding employment, he asked if I drove a car, tractor or other machinery. When I assured him that I had done so, he said, "Good," and sent me with a note to another office in another building, and wished me luck.

The next interview was very informal, with the plant crane supervisor. He was a real down-to-earth sort, whom I liked right away. He also asked about driving and operating machinery, and seemed confident that I would do well running an overhead crane. He wanted me to start the following week, if possible, and gave me a temporary identification tag that would allow me into his particular building.

One problem, as yet unsolved, was obtaining a place to room and board. Dad had previously gotten the address of some relatives of people up in our area, who might provide this service. We found their residence on Heldeberg Avenue, and after a short interview, I was welcomed into their home. I agreed to return on the following weekend with my luggage, and to get to the plant on Monday. My room—shared with their two-year-old son—meals, and bag lunch, would set me back $10 a week!

I had three days to get my affairs in order and return to Schenectady. Between Junior and Dad, my custodial work would be done, along with any other chores for which I was responsible. I needed to purchase a few personal items and some additional clothing, which was readily accomplished.

When I arrived at my boarding house on Saturday, I found that two other employees from up north were also staying there, and had been working at G.E. for some time. "Red" and Ann were accommodating and pleasant hosts. They and the others made me feel right at home, and I enjoyed their company.

On Monday, I took a bus to the G.E. entrance, found my supervisor in his office, and finished filling out the necessary forms. I was then issued a permanent company identification and ushered to my first crane in the turbine department. This was miniature compared with the ones I had noticed rolling back and forth overhead, but I would be up there too in the near future! I would be working nine hours a day, six days a week.

With Christmas only two weeks away, I began to wonder about getting home, but with a three-day layoff, Red and Ann were going north and were glad to take me along. It seemed good to get home, especially at this time. After a delightful holiday, I returned to Schenectady with my new friends, and was back to work on Monday.

In the next eleven months, I progressed to the larger overhead and gantry cranes, and received salary increases and benefits. During that time, I bought a 1935 Ford club coupe that Red had traded in on a new 1940 model, for $125. I also bought the family some new appliances, through G.E., a new split-bamboo fly rod, and a .16 gauge over-and-under shotgun. Being interested in flying, I took some flying lessons at Round Lake, in a Piper Cub on floats.

Having a car of my own allowed me to go home once in awhile, when it was possible to get away. In the latter part of the year, I went on a night shift in the cable department, which gave me days to have some recreation, and kept me out of the night spots where I wasn't comfortable anyway. I spent most of my days outdoors, fishing, flying or riding horseback. But this prosperity was short-lived, for my name had come up for the Selective Service in mid-November. Uncle Sam wasted no time getting me into the U.S. Army, where I spent the next four years.

Junior and I were very close as brothers, and during our military service we sometimes came within 20,000 feet of each other—he as a crew member of a B-24, based in England—and me as a Field Artillery Supply Officer in France!

The many varied experiences over those twenty odd years gave me an expanded awareness for the future. The lessons of youth, learn all you can, while you can, have served us well. As an adult you realize that you have had a good life—a full life—guided by the perseverance and love of family and friends.